AF379341

pegging the wind

The Red Moon Anthology
of English-Language Haiku
2002

Jim Kacian ✧ Editor-in-Chief

Ernest J. Berry ✧ Tom Clausen
Ellen Compton ✧ D. Claire Gallagher
Maureen Gorman ✧ A. C. Missias
Kohjin Sakamoto ✧ Alan Summers
George Swede ✧ Max Verhart

pegging the wind:
The Red Moon Anthology of
English-Language Haiku 2002

© 2003 by Jim Kacian
for Red Moon Press
All Rights Reserved

ISBN 978-1-893959-32-3

Red Moon Press
P. O. Box 2461
Winchester VA
22604-1661 USA
www.redmoonpress.com

All work published in
by permission of the individual authors
or their accredited agents.

Cover painting: Jacob Kainen, *The Vulnerable*
1954, 42" x 50", oil on canvas.
Ruth Cole Kainen Collection.
Used by permission.

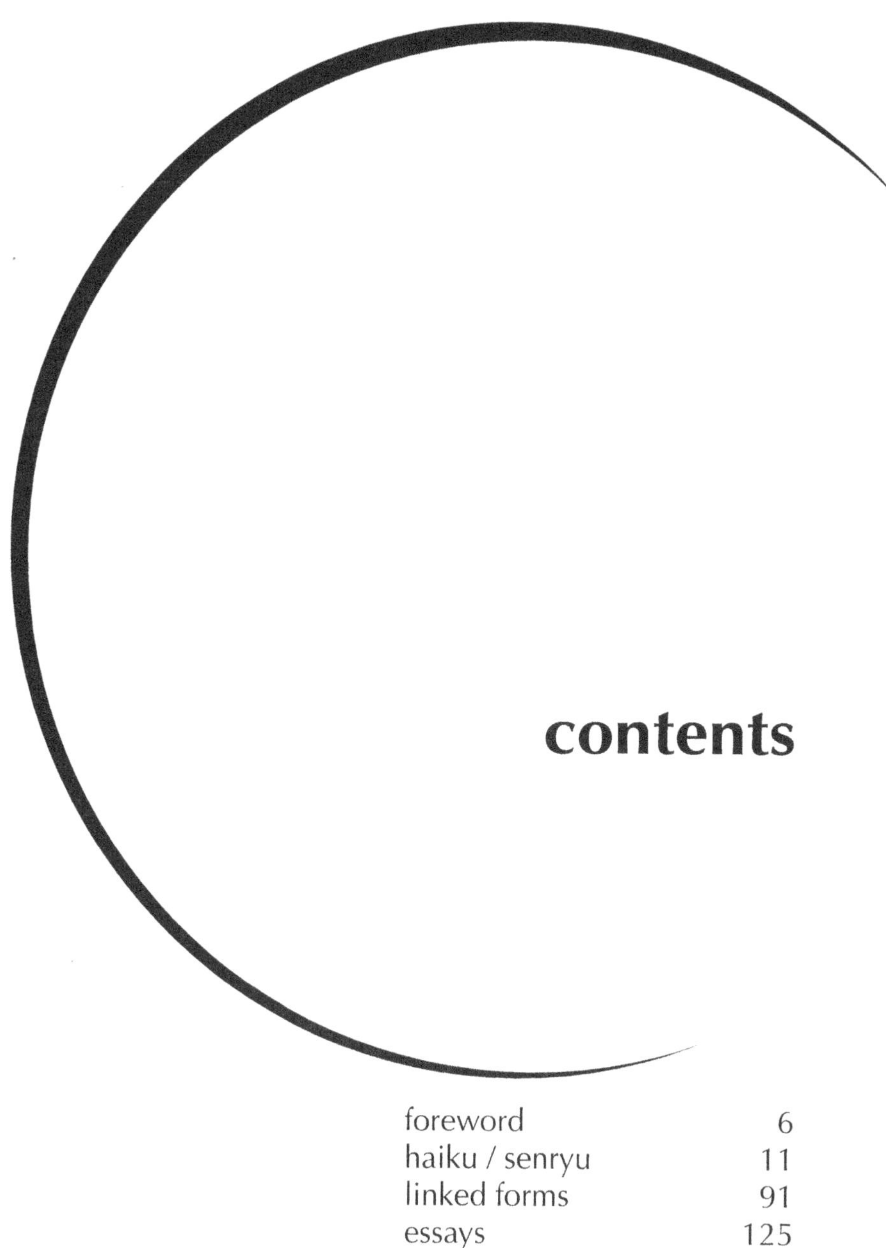

contents

foreword

Red Moon Press enters its tenth year with the publication of this volume, our seventh Red Moon Anthology. In our early years our ambition was simply to publish a haiku journal, and creating a press seemed a useful step towards helping manage the process.

We have been extremely fortunate along the way, attracting the best poets working in haiku and related fields to appear in our pages. Our first book was The Red Moon Anthology 1996, the inaugural volume of what has become the flagship publication of the press. Our first individual collection was endgrain by Dee Evetts, which has become a collector's item. Our first book of theory was the first volume of H. F. Noyes' Favorite Haiku series. All these, and nearly all our other publications, have gone on to win awards from critics and accolades from readers.

Since those early days we have produced other anthologies, other individual and specialty collections, other books of theory and criticism, even a haiku novel. But it is the Red Moon Anthology which has always defined our press, and will continue to do so. It is within these pages that we offer not only a review of the accomplishments of the haiku world year by year, but also help establish the standard for excellence in our genre. It has been written many times and in many places, that ppearance herein constitutes the highest compliment a contemporary haiku in English can receive. Of course we're delioghted to be so perceived, and take it as a challenge to keep improving the volume, in terms both of content and physical product.

None of this would matter, or even exists, of course, without you, our discerning readers and patrons. Thank you. We look forward to another ten years—and more—of sharing our love of haiku with you.

Jim Kacian
Editor-in-Chief

pegging the wind

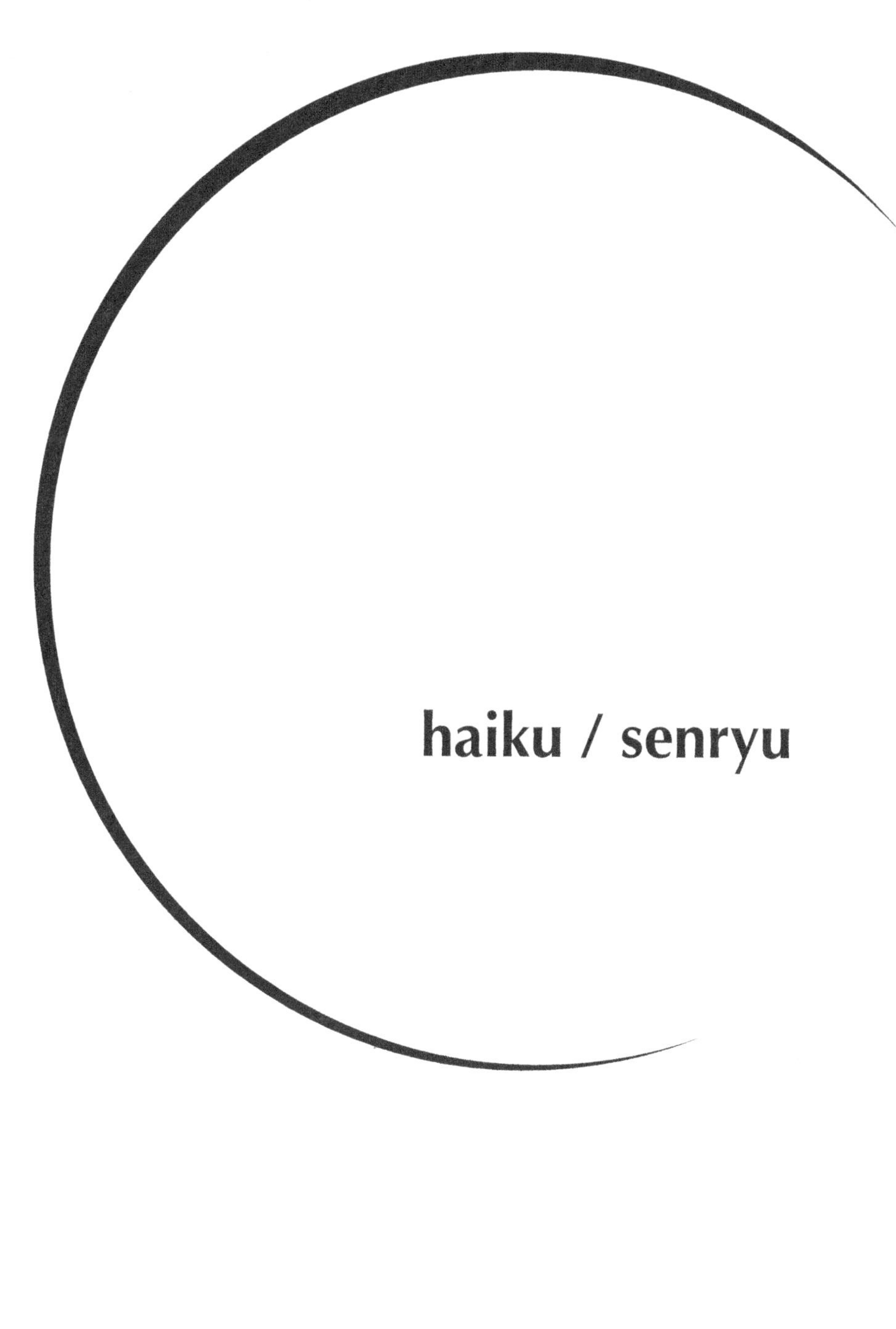

haiku / senryu

Astrid Andreescu ✧ United States

nursing home —
a man in a wheelchair
by the parrot cage

Stephen Atkinson ✧ England

on the memorial
to the dead of two world wars
my name

Nick Avis ✧ Canada

the dada exhibit
a tourist photographs
the exit sign

Pamela A. Babusci ✧ United States

snow-covered village . . .
i follow a stranger's footprints
over the bridge

Francine Banwarth   ✧   United States

first night of snow
sifting through
his box of old buttons

Johnny Baranski   ✧   United States

Prison lights out
drifting off to distant places
a train whistle

John Barlow ✧ England

skinning squid
the deep-tanned hands
of the fisherman

Jack Barry ✧ United States

strangers' voices—
stopping in mid-call
hermit thrush

Nicholas Barwell ✦ Australia

reverie
quiet snip of scissors
in the barber shop

Roberta Beary ✦ United States

third date
the slow drift of the rowboat
in deep water

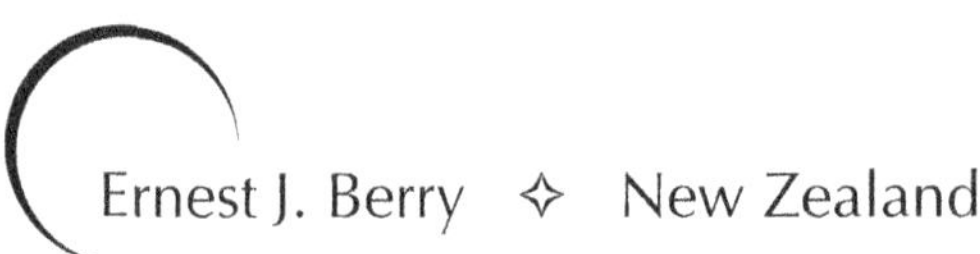

Ernest J. Berry ✧ New Zealand

doorbell
my thoughts
dress up

desert heat
the lizard disappears
into a snake

Mykel Board ✧ United States

not showing up—
the woman I wanted
to snub

Harry Bose ✧ United States

deep in the woods—
all the shadows bend
toward home

Patricia Bostian ✧ United States

arguing in bed—
half your face in moonlight
half in the dark

Mark Brooks ✧ United States

autumn mist
my neighbor goes inside
without a word

Randy M. Brooks ✧ United States

> 25th anniversary . . .
>   she sits on the suitcase
>   to zip it shut

Greba Brydges-Jones ✧ New Zealand

> monday
> pegging the wind
> into our sheets

Owen Bullock ✧ New Zealand

ex-junkie
two bags
in his teacup

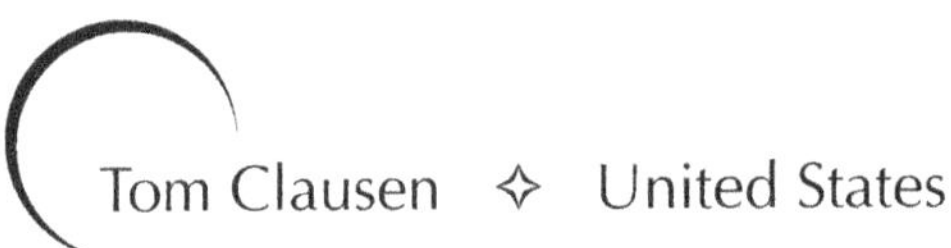

Tom Clausen ✧ United States

turning it down
at the red light
—oldies station

Yu Chang ✧ United States

end of the walk
she tells me how
she divorced her ex-

happy hour
my son and I
piling up mussels

Kathy Lippard Cobb ✧ United States

spring breakup—
I explain that monogamy
is not a board game

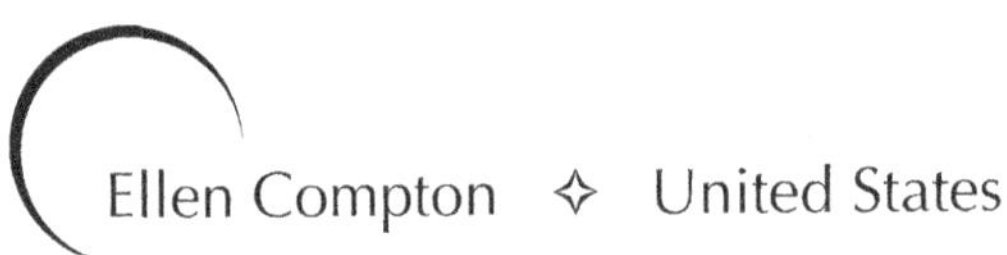

Ellen Compton ✧ United States

winter storm watch
the stock pot
comes to a boil

john crook ✦ England

fifth birthday
feeling the new gap
with her tongue

William Cullen Jr. ✦ United States

first snow
staring at the monkey cage
the homeless man

DeVar Dahl ✧ Canada

old garden shed—
morning glories climb
the bicycle spokes

Susan Delphine Delaney ✧ United States

sipping champagne
listening to the tiny sounds
of living alone

Kristen Deming ✧ United States

shifting
with the shifting sands—
desert land mines

Angelee Deodhar ✧ India

haiga workshop
in the downstroke of the brush
the sound of rain

Andrew Detheridge ✧ England

quiet enough
to hear the squirrel
change his grip

Vladimir Devidé ✧ Croatia

New Year's Day.
The snowman in a new
coat of snow.

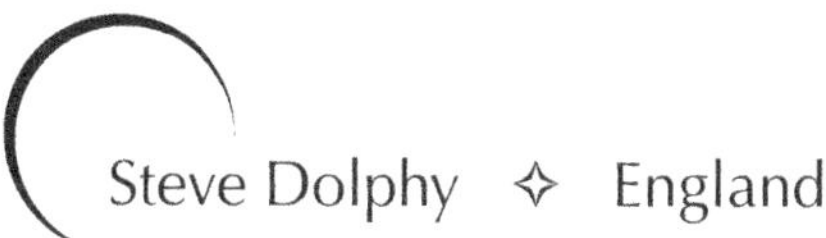

Steve Dolphy ✧ England

temple rockpool
a tadpole swims
from dark to light

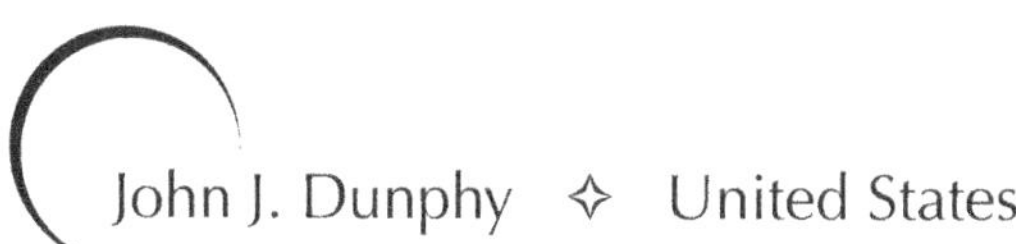

John J. Dunphy ✧ United States

war crimes trial
the defendant tries to suppress
another yawn

David Elliott ✧ United States

January storm—
    taking down the porch bell
to get some sleep

Robert Epstein ✧ United States

Each swig
of the bottled water
the sky

Michael L. Evans ✧ United States

Agate Beach
finally finding one
in a gift shop

Dee Evetts ✧ United States

recycling day
I stare at headlines
from September 10th

Basem Farid ✧ England

Boxing Day
estranged couple
exchange children

Ross Figgins ✧ United States

empty kitchen
passing moonlight shines
on a faded calendar

Janice Fixter ✧ England

talking in his sleep
he finishes the quarrel
with his brother

Muriel Ford ✧ Canada

a cold wind blows
blank space on the headstone
at my parents' grave

Stanford M. Forrester ✧ United States

cereal box . . .
the toy submarine
at the bottom

Marco Fraticelli ✧ Canada

seniors residence
waiting for the elevator door
to close

D. Claire Gallagher   ✧   United States

after love
this sweet burst
of cherry tomato

nine-month belly—
she slowly unwraps
the heirloom crêche

Garry Gay ✧ United States

Floating mist
she gathers goose eggs
in a porcelain bowl

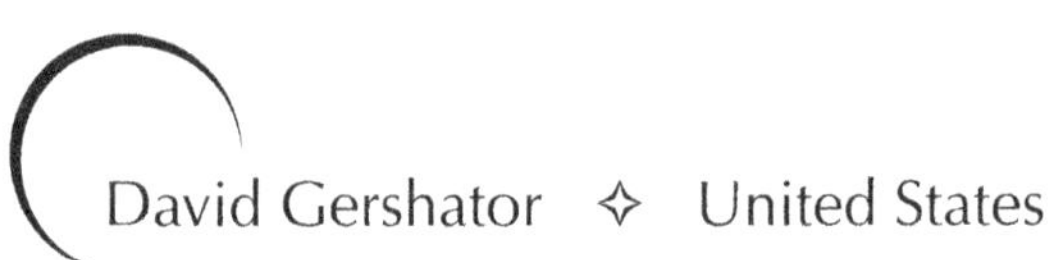

David Gershator ✧ United States

on hold . . .
staring at the sea
until I'm disconnected

Nigel Gibbons ✧ England

> farmyard track—
> the old dog lies down
> after one bark

Ferris Gilli ✧ United States

> first azaleas
> the cat widens a rip
> in the screen door

Ria Giskes-Pieters ✧ Netherlands

one by one
the trees of the forest
in the fog

Ann Goldring ✧ United States

january thaw
our snowman
heads for the creek

LeRoy Gorman ✦ Canada

all day rain
two parts water
one part scotch

Kay Grimnes ✦ United States

first snow
the baby's fingers
closer around nothing

Lee Gurga ✧ United States

summer harbor—
each boat pointing
to the storm

Carolyn Hall ✧ United States

smiling through tears
exactly the haircut
I asked for

Yvonne Hardenbrook ✧ United States

solstice afternoon
the ice-cube in my tea
turns over

Jeffrey Harpeng ✧ New Zealand

twilight drizzle—
at the accident scene
scattered oranges

Christopher Herold ✧ United States

Mt. St. Helens—
on the visitor center lawn
fresh mole hills

Cicely Hill ✧ England

midnight lightning
neighbour never seen before
there at her window

Gary Hotham ✧ United States

a late arrival
in the back row—
the odor of rain

no name for his illness—
the plastic lid snaps back on
the coffee can

the sun's warmth
part of the house
we seldom use

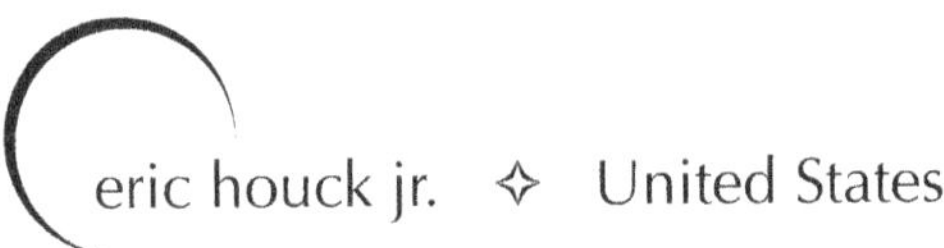

eric houck jr. ✧ United States

the same old tom
pissing on the same old tire
winter solstice

Elizabeth Howard ✧ United States

hum of the wheel
potter's cupped brown hands
rising

Joyce Sandeen Johnson ✧ United States

cycling
faster than we can pedal
the storm

Ken Jones ✧ Wales

Three Minute Silence
bird song
        and some deeper grief

Jim Kacian ✧ United States

three-quarter moon—
imagining she can feel it
move inside her

a letter from a prisoner—
the wide spaces
between words

cemetery
the sharp edges
of the new names

Kirsty Karkow ✧ United States

alone again
. . . the last raspberry
sharp on my tongue

Michael Ketchek ✧ United States

windstorm
the Christmas lights
tangled with the flag

M. Kettner ✧ United States

your hair drawn back
the sharp tastte of radishes

Joann Klontz ✧ United States

country road
the pothole filler
works alone

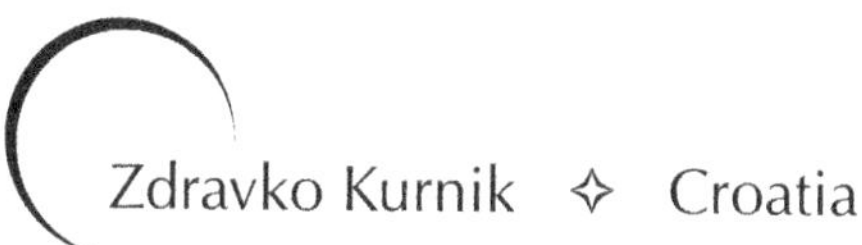

Zdravko Kurnik ✧ Croatia

forest path
for half an hour two snails
passing each other

Sean Lausé ✧ United States

after the rain
a spider
weaving suns

Lori Laliberte-Carey ✧ United States

baggage claim
two women compare
their swelling wombs

heavy traffic
the route sign covered
with honeysuckle

rising moon
the snowman stands
with open arms

Leo Lavery ✧ Northern Ireland

wrong number
back bare-arsed
to the bathroom

Angela Leuck ✧ Canada

after winter
the fountain flowing—
we speak of your dead son

Martin Lucas ✧ England

the echo behind
the chanting of monks . . .
folded clouds

paul m. ✧ United States

back again—
the driftwood thrown
with all my strength

Patricia Machmiller ✧ United States

the remaining snow
in isolated patches
our separate lives

Makiko ✧ United States

flea market
a keen appraisal
of the frame

Giovanni Malito ✧ Ireland

late May sun . . .
sharing a birthday
with this butterfly

midweek rain . . .
slicing away mold
from the bread

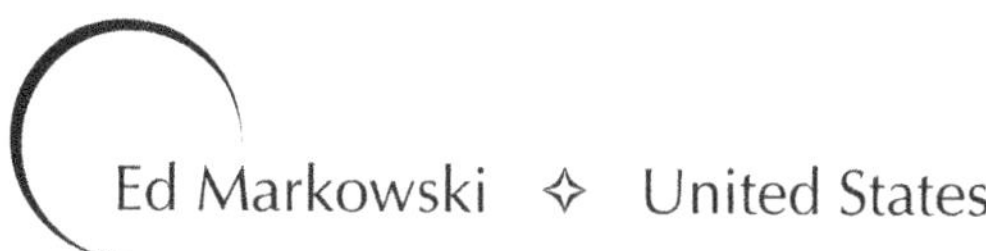

Ed Markowski ✧ United States

Charity ball
limousines long enough
to live in

Steve Mason ✧ England

prison wall a sparrow under the razor wire

Valerie Matsumoto ✦ United States

knowing your cough
but not your face —
invalid neighbor

Michael McClintock ✦ United States

walking home
by a new path
mint leaves

Dorothy McLaughlin ✧ United States

husband and wife
across from each other
playing solitaire

Paul David Mena ✧ United States

hot summer night—
following a bead of sweat
between her breasts

Sue Mill ✧ Australia

evensong
the cool silence
between chants

A. C. Missias ✧ United States

summer evening:
a sparrow works
the sidewalk cracks

Matt Morden   ✧   Wales

first day of spring
the spider's web starts
at the axe handle

Naia   ✧   United States

tumbling snowflakes
I lose my thoughts to the space
between deck planks

Pamela Miller Ness   ✧   United States

shifting clouds
I twist
my wedding ring

another hot day
an old man scratches
his lottery ticket

in remission—
bidding high
at the auction sale

Ayaz Daryl Nielsen ✧ United States

a single man's thoughts—
beneath the ice
a lone mitten

H. F. Noyes ✧ Greece

subway posters—
the stares of missing children
grow familiar

Marian Olson ✧ United States

with just enough light
to woo her
firefly

withered,
persimmons he didn't have time
to pick
(for Kenneth C. Leibman)

Mukai Otaka ✧ Japan

A firefly
lights up the life lioine
on my palm.

Christopher Patchel ✧ United States

tall grass
both teams lose track
of the score

w. f. owen ✧ United States

bare trees
another negative
pregnancy test

day's end
reaching the edge
of the map

Tom Painting ✧ United States

password
his ex-wife's name
opens a file

spring plowing
a flock of blackbirds
turns inside out

piper   ✧   United States

wishing fountain
outside the cancer clinic:
some heads, some tails

Tony Pupello   ✧   United States

talk of separation
I gather the Easter eggs
back in the basket

K. Ramesh   ✧   India

a yellow leaf
touching the green ones
on its way down

Emily Romano   ✧   United States

death watch
her knitting needles keeping
silence at bay

Linda Robeck ✧ United States

For Sale sign
after eight years
meeting the neighbors

menstruation
the child we talk
and talk of having

Gabriel Rosenstock ✧ Ireland

Cry of seagulls:
fish-vendors testing
the knife's edge

Bruce Ross ✧ United States

spring morning
the shadow of a building
on a building

Charles Rossiter ✧ United States

bordertown motel:
another movie not good enough
to watch at home

Philip Rowland ✧ Japan

the table
without the tablecloth—
autumn evening

Timothy Russell ✧ United States

zen garden
bees disassemble
a monarch butterfly

Eric Rutter ✧ United States

mad again
her silence fills
the silence

Edin Saracevic ✧ Slovenia

sharpening the axe –
the wind brings
the smell of snow

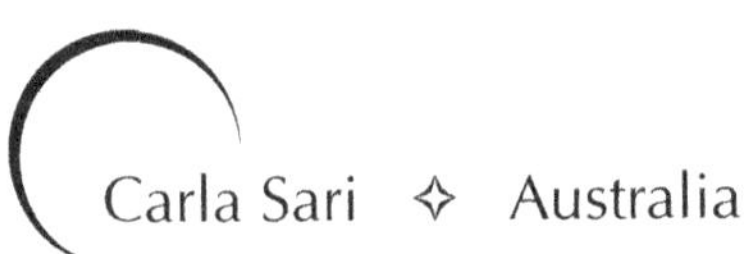

Carla Sari ✧ Australia

school graffiti
the four letter word
spelled correctly

Grant Savage ✧ Canada

psych ward
moonlight
climbs the walls

light in the wings
of the shadow
of a dragonfly

Rob Scott ✧ Netherlands

icemelt—
the moon drifts
through my whisky

Yasuhiko Shigemoto ✧ Japan

The sunset glow—
Hiroshima
as if still burning

Andrew Shimield ✧ England

Up escalator—
the morning faces
looking down

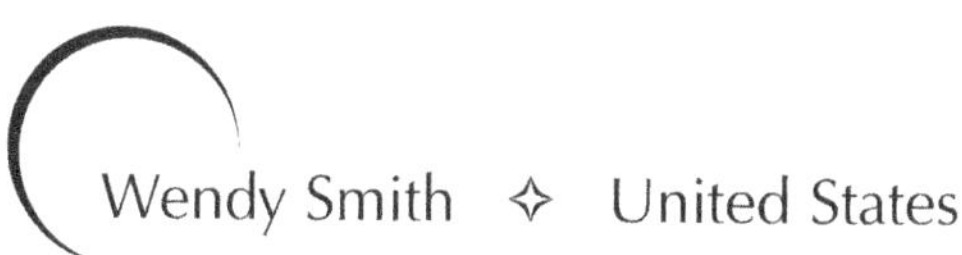

Wendy Smith ✧ United States

winter
in a world of one color
the taste of peaches

Robert Spiess ✦ United States

an old folks home
on a trellis
    evening glories

Dan Spurgeon ✧ United States

new boots—
I choose
the unshoveled path

Elizabeth St Jacques   ✧   Canada

home from hospital—
spinning the bicycle wheel
just for its sound

Lynne Steel   ✧   United States

Easter morning
someone else has left
flowers on his grave

David Steele ✧ England

stuck to the slab
the   i
of the frozen f sh

R. A. Stefanac ✧ United States

because he asked
blowing soap bubbles
at his graveside

John Stevenson ✧ United States

        fireworks
        I close my eyes
        for a second look

        jampackedelevatoreverybuttonpushed

        applauding
        the mime
        in our mittens

George Swede ✧ Canada

in mother's room
only the photos of the dea
dust free

airport lounge
a Muslim man prays toward
the emergency exit

in the pawnshop window
a hooker studies
her reflection

Patrick Sweeney   ✧   Japan

Rainy
season
the
silent
treatment
ends

Anna Tambour   ✧   Australia

preoccupied—
my hand fills with
dog nose

Maurice Tasnier ✧ England

assertiveness class
the newcomer
rearranging chairs

a few cross words
he rearranges
the window cacti

old love letters
the elastic band
shriveling

Hilary Tann ✧ United States

fumbling
with tenses
at the wake

Cindy Tebo ✧ United States

horsetail clouds
a field of sky
without fences

D. A. Thomann   ✧   United States

jail time
the new guy still
sunburnt

Tom Tico   ✧   United States

With my mother gone
faces I'll never identify
in the family album

Serge Tomé ✦ Belgium

open air market
cheese and people
of all scents

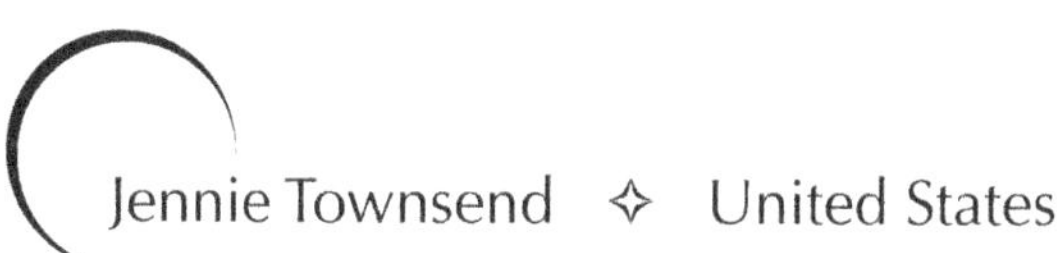

Jennie Townsend ✦ United States

day's end
a bit of clover
floats in the bath

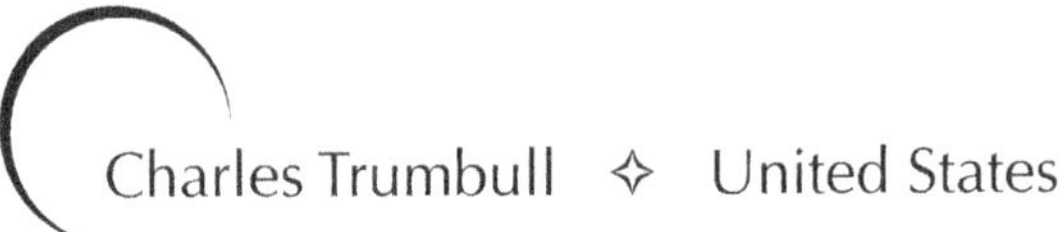

Charles Trumbull ✧ United States

September chill:
the groundsman's tractor
coughs into life

Richard von Sturmer ✧ New Zealand

hot day in Kyoto
people pass by the God of Wind
fanning themselves

Tomislav Z. Vujcic ✧ Yugoslavia

in prison
spring rain takes me back
to my youth

J. Marcus Weekley ✧ United States

fairy dress
in the display window
Salvation Army

Michael Dylan Welch ✧ United States

> morning sun—
>   a patch of frost
> in the holstein's shadow

Alan Wells ✧ New Zealand

> At the end of its leaf
> the inchworm, feeling
> for a foothold on the wind

Peter Williams ✧ England

autumn wind
a paperboy chases
the news

piano recital
someone's cough
broadcast to the nation

Bill Wyatt ✧ England

On the telephone
a voice from the distant past —
early winter rain

Ruth Yarrow ✧ United States

lift off
in my belly the pull
of earth

Mitsuko Yusa ✧ Japan

An evening cicada—
slowly pouring water
on the unwashed rice

Cindy Zackowitz ✧ United States

a damp evening—
each of us with
our own cloud of gnats

Alenka Zorman ✧ Croatia

my husband away—
I arrange our slippers
more carefully

Edward Zuk ✧ Canada

the harvest moon —
a cabbage moth resting
on the tractor

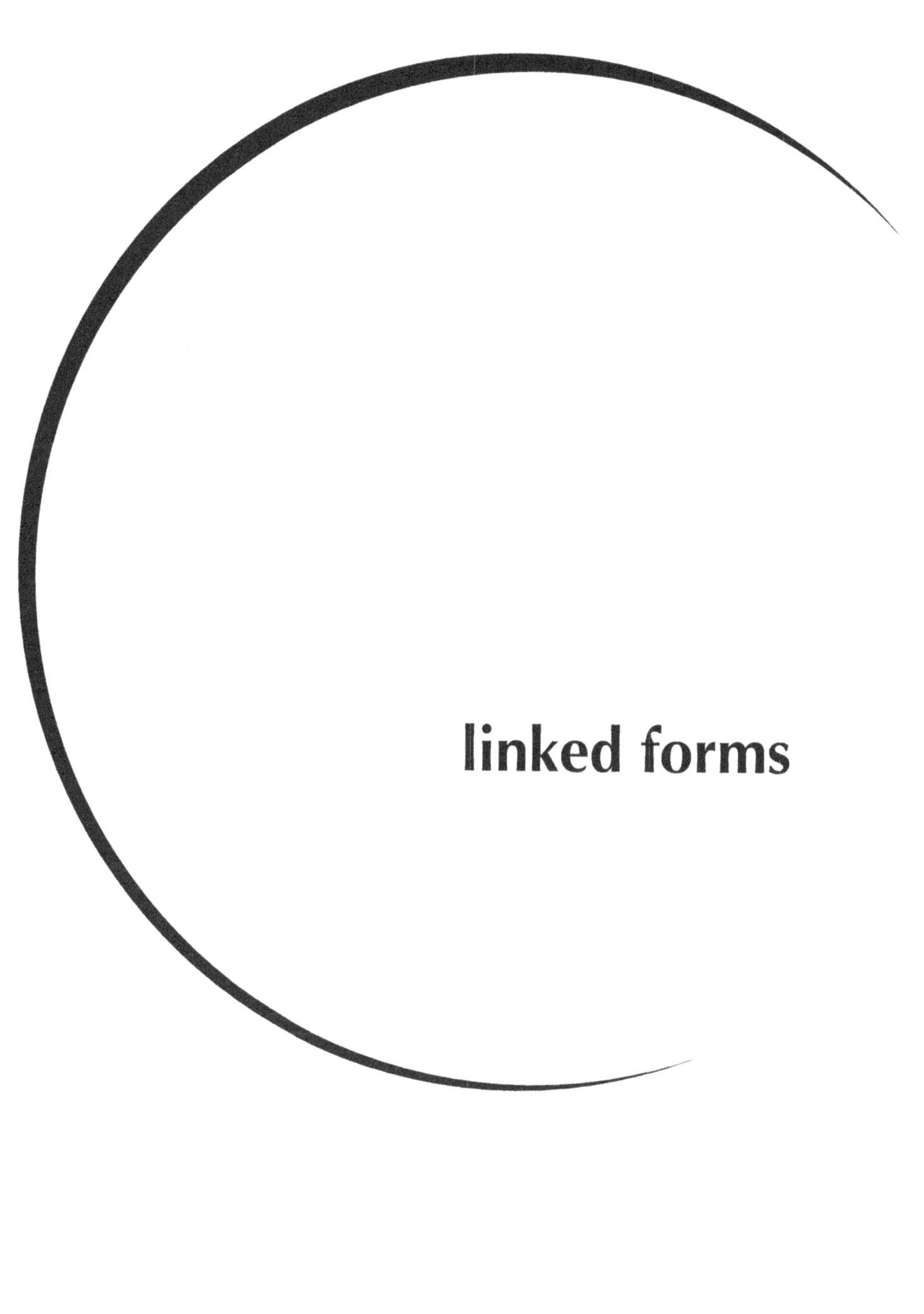
linked forms

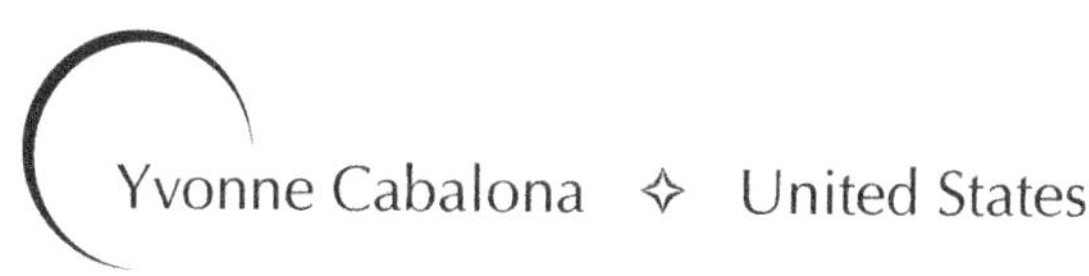

Yvonne Cabalona ✧ United States

Deep Winter

In the late 80s, I was taking a course on human sexuality at the local junior college. One of the topics addressed was AIDS and the instructor informed us she had invited a young man afflicted with the illness to our next session. Despite fighting a cold, I was eager to attend, though several classmates chose not to, including a young pregnant woman who felt that breathing the same air as the AIDS victim was dangerous and could cause her to lose her baby.

I don't remember his name or where he said he came from. It was apparent he had once been very handsome. In spite of the room's warmth, he never took off his coat. Once introduced, he told us he would answer any questions we had except those regarding his family—he had been disowned. His vulnerability was palpable.

We knew AIDS was fatal; our curiosity was in homosexuality. We asked about that. One of the rare times he smiled was when he spoke about San Francisco. Listening to his story, a sudden insight came to me—I realized he was more in danger of catching my virus that I was of catching his.

> deep winter
> I time my breathing
> with his

Del Doughty ✧ United States

Haibun

Nine at night I'm in line to buy to buy diapers at Kroger. The old coule ahead of me in their moldy clothes counting browned pennies. The clerk, his eyes averted, tells them "no," not enough, and the old folks fumble a moment, chuckle an apology, throw their loaf of bread off the conveyor belt. I offer to float them the difference, but no, they say, we've gotta go, and they scamper out of the store, their step quick as the nip in the evening air.

My turn. The clerk scans my diapers and recites the price. I'd like, I say, to buy those folks that loaf of bread. The clerk snaps his hand and gives the command to the bagger to go and fetch a new loaf. But isn't it just right here? I say, motioning under the counter. The clerk shows me the loaf he'd thrown in the trash. "Store policy," he says. I shrug and hand him a Hamilton.

waiting for my change—
the store clerk and I talk
about the wind

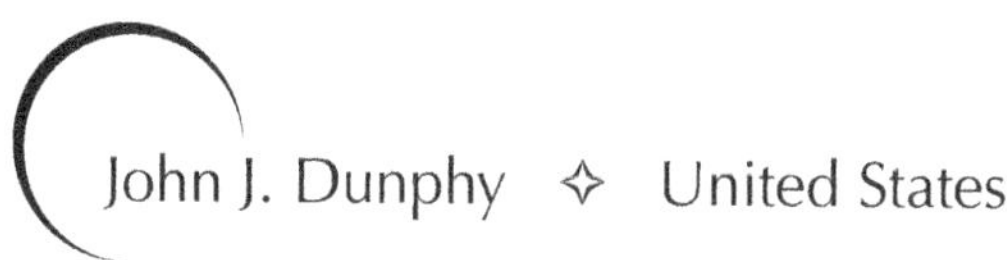

John J. Dunphy ✧ United States

Batterered Customers

My book shop's original location was two doors away from a shelter for battered women. To ensure the security of its temporary residents, no sign identified the building. Of course, I was always painfully aware of its existence.

Many times I saw women, frequently accompanied by their children, emerge from cabs or police cars and enter the building. Occasionally the woman carried a suitcase. More often, she and her children had only the clothes on their backs.

When thesse women learned that my book shop was a safe place and that I would never betray their whereabouts, they stopped by to browse and temporarily forget the misery that forced them to seek refuge at the shelter. Even after so many years, I still recall particular customers.

on reading a joke book
her bruised face
tries to smile

Judson Evans ✧ United States

The Word For It

The brush burn of shame, when my brother walked in on me wrestling another boy my age, our swimsuits around our ankles and he "knew the word for it." Then the woods after school green branch of yew drawn across the white belly, the pruned wands of dogwood touched and retouched bodies uninflected still cloud-like with new names or pressed against the barrels in the dry heat of the barn where piles of rotting flags burned without flame or the padlocked nursery shed where the leaking bags of lime burned throat and nostrils the muffled friction like the tumblers in a safe . . .

> under the railway bridge
> broken stalks of jewelweed
> bead with sap

I worked to impress them, the older boys, jammed the pistachio machine in the Laundromat with a screwdriver and filled the lining of my coat with lint-covered coins, bought a knife like theirs, put my hand on the target for a dare. Body of lapses and lucid elisions, the scar between my fingers, the suddenly opened door, the balsa light cone of laminations . . . When I fell two stories down from the oak outside

my window, my body broke its promise in the hottest
August's days, teeth clenched on the metal taste the
sweat seemed to come from . . .

    summer thunder
    slow knit of bone
    beneath the cast

Marco Fraticelli ✧ Canada
Carolyne Rohrig ✧   United States

Ash Wednesday

with the kindling
I bring in
dead wasps

    her remains
    still on the mantel

Valentine's day
a black and white movie
on TV

    fish market
    wrapping the day's catch
    in yesterday's paper

fingerprints
on the Mother's Day card

    Ash Wednesday
    a smudge
    on the baby's forehead

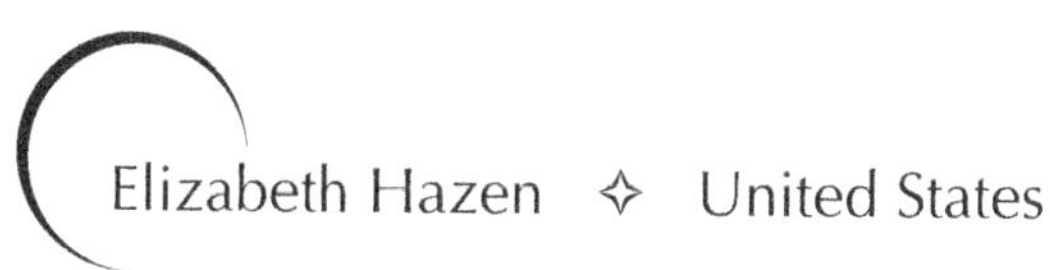

Elizabeth Hazen   ✧   United States

Shadows Cross

I leave the trail and climb to a mossy outcrop not far away. From here I can watch the woods. A three-inch millipede passes. Another. Another. Eleven.

    a thousand feet
    above sea level
    wild columbine

Below me a red fox trots along the trail I just left. Scarcely a minute later a man and dog go the opposite way, walking in the very footprints.

    empty snake skin
    the tips of ferns
    still curled

Nothing happens. Dog and man miss the fox. Dog and man and fox miss me. The millipedes miss each other and the rest of us. Perhaps we are all on different planes.

    trail of birch pollen
    bird shadows cross
    each other

Ken Jones ♦ Wales

The Spirit Level

In this life
we walk on the roof of hell
and view the flowers
Kobayashi Issa

"Next Wednesday—we'll phone the results to you between 4 and 45. Do you understand?"

After the biopsy, sweet coffee in a styrofoam cup. Driving home the familiar sunny hills are restless now with my unease. Five days to go. Five days to finish the summer house. Wednesday dawns fine.

Coiling and drifting smoke
from a new-lit fire
sunbright blue

Just enough worn old bricks to build the steps. I watch myself loading the barrow with slow deliberation. Cement, buckets, the clatter of this and that. And the long bright spirit level. The mortar mix—not too stiff, not too sloppy. This trowelling of mortar is balm to the spirit. I lay the level across the finished slabs. The spirit bubble sits dead center, between its two hair lines. How could it be otherwise? it says.

She has set out our lunch with care. Two polished glasses filled with sunlight; two white napkins rather

unnerving. 3o'clock. I potter at my desk. Outside, she
listens to a neighbour who has been touched by Jesus.
The dark green phone waits, silent in its cradle and
unbelievable when it rings.

> So sorry. It's cancer —
> I go wring out the washing
> hang it out to dry

Back to the summer house, trying not to disturb the
new steps. Lock the door. Listen to the wind.

From west to east we flee together. To where the
sun rises up from the sea instead of sinking into it. To
where the world shrinks to a thin line between sky
and fen. At Southwold, ppints of Adnam's "Broadside"
bitter. A jar of white honey from the Walberswick
hives. Matins at Ely; evensong at Norwich.

> Blackened niche
> last year's nest
> where a saint once stood

Home for more tests. The radiology unit has an air
of carnival. What shall we play for you?

> Bone scan
> the length
> of a Brandenburg Concerto

Judgement Day, at 11:30 am. Yama, the bug-eued
Lord of Death, turns out to be a breezy fellow, an old
school tie bright against his white coat. Obsequies
sseriously postponed. They can "help me live" at

least until the end of the decade. I could even end up dying of something better. We celebrate at the Owl & Pussycat Tea-room. Sipping Earl Grey, I number the hairs of my head.

Returning home, we find visitors —

Into the sadness
a pair of mating ducks
alighting on our pond

Dedicated to fellow haijin John Crook, who died of cancer 16 April 2001.

Jim Kacian ✧ United States

beneath a waxing moon

I pare my nails and toss the white crescents into the fire, scenting the air faintly, unmistakeably human.

camping alone
the crackle of dry twigs
in the fire

Jim Kacian ✧ United States

Eastertide

On a recent late Saturday afternoon, after a day in boats on the sea, I accompanied a friend to church. While he made his confession I strolled the periphery of the old building. In alcoves where the Stations of the Cross, the synoptic 14-stage story of Christ's accusation, trial and crucifixion, had once been placed now stood nothing but moldy, crumbling plaster. The gloomy light of the votive candles, the rarified slant of winter sun through stained glass, the muted ambience of high-vaulted ceilings conspired to make of this absence a felt emptiness. I felt oddly chastened, the more so for the purple raiment of the altar linen, the smells of beeswax and frankincense and worn wood, and transported to the chiaroscuro of my childhood, who had just reveled in the broad horizons and sharp salt smells, the clear sky and endless depths of sea that have become the arenas of my prodigal life.

> just a fluke
> returning to the deep . . .
> do I believe in God?

Kirsty Karkow ✧ United States
Maria Steyn ✧ South Africa

Cheek to Cheek

sundried track
the pinto pony canters
in waltz time

garden steps
moonlight on her ballgown

circling the fire
Apache braves opffer
a peace pipe

flute lesson
a yellow leaf twirls
outside the window

dancing with the teacher
cheek to cheek

Nutcracker Suite
the smile in his eyes
as the curtain lifts

Wim Lofvers ✦ Netherlands

Haibun

I must have been about ten years old, when, one day, my mother took me to the lake, where we walked along the reeds of the shore. It was a glorious spring day, shortly before mowing time; the grass grew knee-high and fields were full of flowers, which smelt wonderfully fresh. Though it was not allowed, we lay down on our backs in the grass. The air was full of the cries of the birds which had theirs nests and young in the vicinity. Loveliest I thought the lark, which soared higher than all the other birds; we could hear its song long after we had lost sight of it in the blue expanse. Why does this moment keep recurring to my mind? My mother died long ago, the lark can no longer be found around our meadows and I myself have become an old and deaf man.

I greet the stump
of the sawn-off tree
in the spring sunshine

Michael McClintock ✧ United States
Michael Dylan Welch ✧ United States

The Lotus Eaters

hefting a plum —
I know by heart
my father's orchard

    downtown library —
    I dare to eat a peach

she takes the apple
from my palm . . .
and it's understood

    blackberry stains
    in the wooden basket —
    knowing she's late

leading down the lane,
crumbs of lemon cake

    languid afternoon —
    I swallow the lotus fruiut
    placed upon my tongue

Michael McClintock ✧ United States

Gangaa-mahaa-nadii

An old woman whose breasts are so long with age they touch the water hyacinths that float at her belly repeats a mantra that was old in the time of Babylon and Thebes.

The rim of the sun is pushing up through haze. With some hurry a few of the others who are here at this early hour remove their outer clothes and place them folded on the stone steps of the ghat beside the mother of rivers.

I do not know what theirs words say, but I listen and hear how the words flow through and through the street sounds: the coughing engines, the opening and closing of windows and doors, a speeding motorbike. The words become a limpid texture, holding a thousand percussions. And so the city in all its forms of cupola, tower and walls askew, awakens from one dream to float on another, made of words.

The air is smoky from the cremations that never end; the smell is a mixture of sandalwood and cut flowers, diesel and shit.

    morning bathers . . .
slow hands that ladle light
shining from the Ganges

Michael McClintock   ✧   United States

Unnatural Amber

1   all day in spring,
      deer cross the high meadow
      into the clouds

I came down from my tiny writing cabin in the mountains to accompany my friend George to the annual "Battle of the Robots" event at a small park in downtown Los Angeles. The place was surrounded by skyscrapers and next to a massive old cathedral. George, who teaches engineering and applied physics at the California Institute of Technology, lures me to the spectacle each spring. The contest engages the minds of students who are likely someday to see Jupiter rise over the frozen oceans of Europa, or to examine strange, broken, wall-like formations far back in some Martian canyon of the Nirgal Vallis rift.

But now, here, they create and fight small robot monstrosities intended to stop, dismember, and destroy other small robot monstrosities, the combat taking place within an area the size and shape of a boxing ring.

"Don't pull that poetic sensitivity crap with me," George says. "You know it fascinates you, but you don't know enough about it to be a pessimist. Each year you try to figure it out, but can't. Your poetic knowledge of the world shudders at the thought of raw conflict. What use is your poetry in this context?"

"Shut the hell up, George."

But he had a point. I thought gloomily of a poem I had written a few weeks back, on a tangent theme:

a shining world—
dew drops for the ducklliong
and the beetle it eats

I'd shown George that poem.

2 We took our seats on high bleachers and watched the mechanical slaughter through opera glasses.

All of the combatant machines appeared to be based on insectoid models, except one. The exception was a beautiful, gleaming white sphere, about eighteen inches in diameter. I searched through the printed program and found its description. It was named "ambeer" and had been made by a team of paleontology, engineering and chemistry students. Its combat strategy was purely defensive and non-violent—simply to sit there and do nothing unless attacked. When touched or jostled by an attacker, Amber's designed response was literally to expectorate glue. Chemically, the glue was approximately that of natural amber—the kind paleontologists love to collect and inspect for the twenty-million-year-old bugs preserved within it. The stuff inside Amber, held in a reservoir, dried to hardness in a few seconds upon exposure to the air. A gyroscope mechanism and a few balanced weights within the sphere controlled the ball's movements; simple sound and motion sensors on the outer surface determined when and in what direction the goo would be expelled from a top-mounted spigot onto an adversary.

"Brilliant," I said, reading the program's description. "It intends to glue its enemies to the floor, or to muck up the moving parts of their weapons!"

George fluttered his eyelids and sneered. "The idea's asinine," he said. "Pacifist philosophy does not translate into the natural world, or into physics."

In the first of five elimination rounds, Amber did well by gluing fast to the floor a mean-looking mechanical grasshopper with ice-pick mandibles. The thing had leapt onto Amber's smooth surface, failed to get a grip, and fell off to its doom. It twitched just a few moments before becoming immobile in a glob of maple-colored, unnatural amber. By winning just that one round, Amber went from one of thirty-two battling robots to one of sixteen.

"Pure luck," said George. The man was clearly surprised.

3   city towers
    brighten and dim
    a gusting wind

The remaining sixteen paired off for the second round. Amber drew a match with a flat, segmented, worm-like device that destroyed its victims by getting under them, then flexing and flipping them over onto their backs. George scowled as we watched Amber handle that little horror with ease, gluing its head to the floor in seconds after the beast's first onslaught; it had no way at all of upsetting a sphere.

Amber was suddenly one of eight finalists. I could see alarm on George's face. His confident world was getting a shake and a goose-feather up the nose.

4   new ones appear
    as other pass—
    spring clouds

A light rain fell as the third round began. Amber was paired off against a monster whose one weapon was a buzz saw on a flexible proboscis-like appendage coming out of the center of a turtle-like body. The monster shot across the floor and cut through Amber like a melon. It was over in seconds—but for both of them. Amber died in a fountain of its own fluid, which likewise gushed over the monster turtle, puiddling it and affixing it firmly to the floor. Officially, the contest beetween the two was a draw; of course, neither machine went on to the next round.

"What did I tell you?" George said, blinking at me. I thought he looked like a turtle at that moment. The rain had ceased; it was sunny again.

"Wait until next year, you gas bag," I said. "A few tweaks, and Amber is going to give you a new lesson in physics, pal. It already has. Do the math."

And of course he knew I was right. Just the concept alone had defeated three-quarters of the field that day. Poetic sensitivity, indeed.

    the hiss
    of a broom
    on wet cement

w. f. owen ✦ United States

Canoe

Threat of rain, I jog to get the mail. Pulling letters from the small rectangular mailbox. Here is a large manila envelope from my hometown in Texas. It is my share of the inheritance from sale of my grandparents' rural home . . . Memories of summers my cousins and I spent there. The add-on back bedroom, with the water cooler that added humidity to the already-sticky Texas nights, where Papa and we grandsons slept. After dawn-to-dusk days helping him mow lawns, we played rock-paper-scissors to see who slept where. The loser got the old single bed so hollowed out we nicknamed it "the canoe." Secretly, I always tried to lose. I liked sleeping in that bed because it gave me a feeling of being held . . . Drops hit the envelope. I lock the mailbox and walk home.

November rain
zipping my coat
all the way up

w. f. owen ♦ United States

September Rain

Every semester students in my interpersonal communication class bring personal objects to share. A college-level "show and tell." I start by sharing a Kennedy half-dollar. My birthday is November 22, 1947. I carry the coin as a reminder of that tragic day in 1963. Students bring family heirlooms, photos, trinkets from trips, guitars and sports objects.

September 12, 2001, the day after the terrorist attacks on the World Trade Center and the Pentagon. Although school was canceled yesterday, classes are held today. In my class, a man shares a mask from Mardi Gras; another shows his cross-country shoes; a woman explains the symbolism of her kickboxing shorts. One student brings a box filled with the ashes of her twenty-year-old cat. Someone asks how he can keep his own cat from wandering off and getting lost. "Put butter on its paws," she says. The cat will find its way home by following the scented paw prints. We laugh together.

September rain
in the rubble
a new shoe

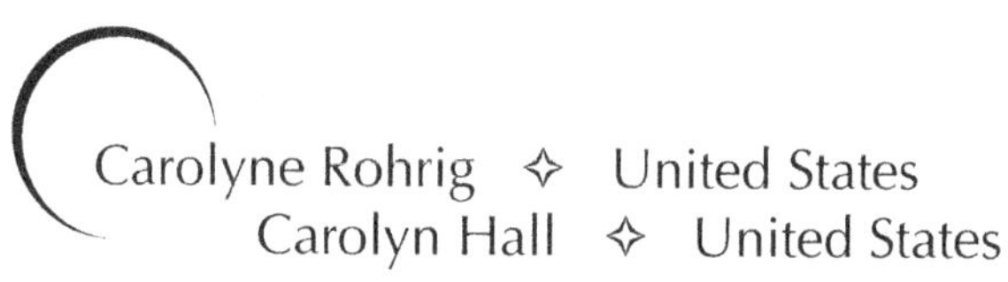

Carolyne Rohrig ✧ United States
Carolyn Hall ✧   United States

Pop Goes the Weasel

children's party
an iridescent bubble
pops over the fence

    all around the mulberry bush
    pop! goes the weasel

after dessert
he pops the question —
"Your room or mine?"

    the ricochet
    of popping corks
    New Year's Eve

climaxing the Pops concert
Beethoven's Ninth

    night-lit stadium
    the hometown slugger
    pops out

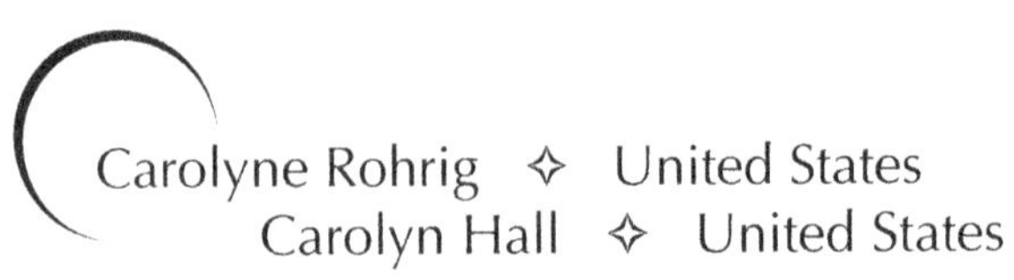

Carolyne Rohrig ✧ United States
Carolyn Hall ✧ United States

Hanging on Every Word

writer's block
inside my favorite book
Acapulco sand

      steamy romance
      two chapters upside down

playground gossip
a little boy hangs
on every word

      tight Scrabble game—
      in her hand
      AAEIIOU

rehearsing the eye chart
before the doctor comes in

      home late again—
      she read him
      the riot act

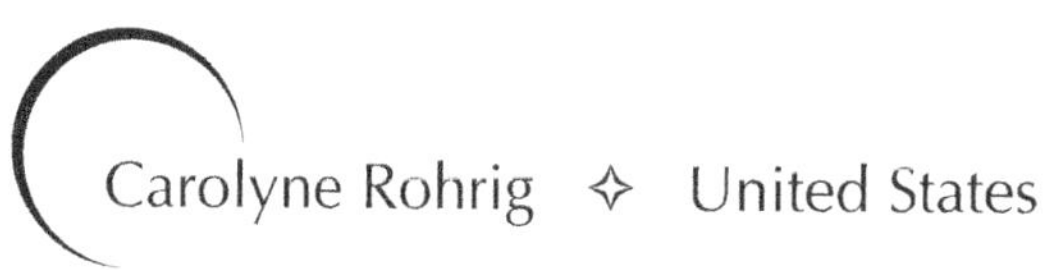

Carolyne Rohrig ✧ United States

Bird on the Wing

I walked into the kitchen and saw her sitting on the back of a chair picking at her bare breast. Her turquoise and yellow feathers had virtually disappeared except for the few that remained around her face and wings. Even her tail was short and stubby. Yet she was happy and quite willing to come onto my arm and continue her pitiful grooming. I asked her owner what trauma caused this and found out she suffered a terrible illness that normally kills macaws, but her life was spared. "I could write a book about all the miracles God did to spare this bird," she said as she came closer in her wheelchair.

winter rain.
last year's pine needles spill
from her umbrella

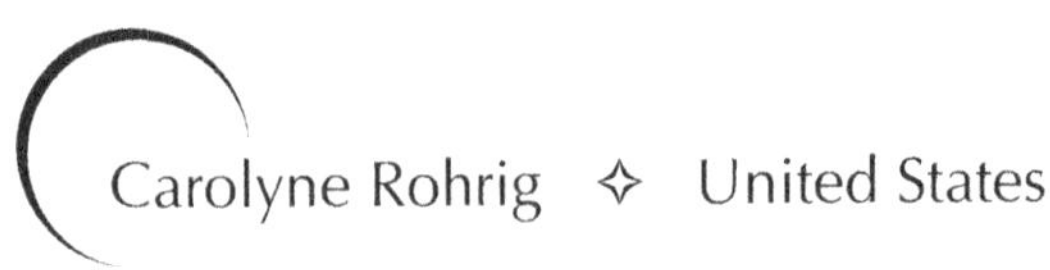

Carolyne Rohrig ✧ United States

In Another Life

It was the mango-colored canaries that drew my attention. I counted six of them. Each bird was in its own small, cramped wooden cage, and each cage was hung at intervals all the way around the courtyard walls of the village hotel. In spite of their confinement, each bird was chirping an exuberant song. Perhaps they were retelling the history of their species and the freedom of the skies they once enjoyed. Or perhaps they sang of the future when one day they might feel the wind currents through their wings and soar over the heights of pyramids again.

old wooden cross—
seeds sprout
in its shadow

Gary Steinberg ✧ United States

Scotch Neat

The nuances of ice: I've learned them well being that all these breakups occur in the depths of winter. There is the irony of fresh snow when it surrounds a house of dis-ease. There is hail, louder than the slamming door. And the cubed ice, clinking inside of "her" vodka. Taken in just the right dosage to numbe "her" pain but never enough to let on who she's been with.

the sound of sleet when there's nothing left to say

Cor van den Heuvel ♦ United States

The Sunbird

September 12, 1998—Saturday. A beautiful warm sunny day in New York City with a blue sky and a few white clouds floating high abovve. Walking down Broadway with seven or eight haiku poets after the Haiku Society of America meeting at Columbia, which had included a lively renku session, I and a few others were stopped by Karen Sohne with "Look—a sundog!" She pointed directly overhead to two or three small wisps of cloud slowly moving eastward.d In one of them a bright spot, or short strip, of yellow was glowing. It seemed to fade and brighten as the wisp slowly flowed and slowly spread out at the same time. It was like a small piece ofd sunset color and yet it wasn't. The color was brighter and more intense than the colors in a sunset. And it was confined to this one small band as if the color were coming from a light source directly within the cloud. Everywhere else above was either blue sky or white clouds.

It was around 5:30 pm and tdhe sun itself was behind the tall buildings (8 to 10 stories high) on the opposite side, the west side, of Broadway. Judging by the sun's glow around the buildings, it was still about 20 to 30 degrees aabove the horizon, somewhere across the river in New Jersey. The wisps of white cloud with the bit of color were a few degrees (3 to 5) south of the zenith as we looked up from the sidewalk, so that although our heads were facing almost straight up, there was a slight tilt towards the southwest. Standing on the east side of Broadway while looking up, we could see that these small clouds, moving towards the buildings next to us, would pass from view above their tops in only a few minutes.

Though the clouds were slowly moving, the strip of colored light stayed in the same place. Yet, because of the cloud's motion, this glowing strip, both in and on the cloud, seemed also to be moving in the opposite direction from one end of the cloud to the other. The wisp of cloud stretched west to east and was very high above us, perhaps 20,000 feet, about where you sometimes see jet liners pass over.

As we watched, the luminous stain changed color, shading into an orange hue, then red. Much deeper and purer than the colors in a rainbow. As it flared and fluttered through shades and tones of red, it seemed to move or jump into the nextd small wisp of clooud. Perhaps the clouod moved into or through this lighted spot, but the original cloud seemed not to have moved completely out of it when the jump occurred. Maybe the spot was a little larger than it appeared. Or it ould be that such phenomena are only visible to the viewer when it can be reflectded from a piece of cloud, or from the condensation, waterdrops, or vapor in the cloud.

In any case it now was in this second wisp which was drifting apart, as the first had done. The red flaring light seemed to pulse and fill with new tints to become a still-changing purple glow. As the cloud wisp came apart the touch of color changed to a pure blue light. The last strands of the cloud seemed to completedly disappear, to evaporate, and now the blue light seemed like a small irregular pool of electric blue in the sky. It was a different kind of blue than the blue sky surrounding it. Almost like a bit of luminous blue ink or paint spilled on a blue table. Then it too was gone.

a rainbow
the little girl lets go
of her balloon

What we saw is not properly called a sundog. I learned this from an interesting book entitled *Rainbows, Mirages and Sundogs* by Roy A. Gallant. Sundogs are related to halos. Halos appear as riings of light around the sun or moon. A "halo," writes Mr. Gallant, "is made by small [ice] crystals positioned every which way. Very small crystals cause a whitish halo with a red edge." He reports that when he's flown through a cloud of these ice crystals, they were "all glittering like miniature diamonds in the sunlight." He add that "They are much smaller than snowflakes and should not be confused with them, or with sleet. A cloud spawning such crystals produces a 22-degree halo along with certain patches and arcs of light. The patches are called sundogs or mock Suns or parhelia."

Most of the time when you see a sundog there will be two of them, one on each side of the halo. They will be at the same height in the sky as the sun. If the sun is on the horizon, the sundogs will be on the rim of the halo. The sundogs will be further out from the rim of the halo the higher the sun is from the horizon.

The author goes on to say that sometimes only

one sundog will be visible and sometimes one or two will appear without the halo. He then describes their appearance. Sundogs are usually "brighter than the halo and may be dazzling. They are clearly red on the inside, with a middle band of yellow that changes to a bluish white part slightly stretched out into a tail that points away from the sun.

After a bit of information about wobbliing and doubling of sundogs we come to a passage that refers in particular to what we saw above Broadway: "An especially beautiful member of the halo family . . . is a brightly colored short curve, or arc, very nearly straight overhead next to the zenith position. Called the circumzenith arc (meaning: arc around the zenith), it is not often observed by most people because so few of us ever look straight up. This lovely arc is visible only when the Sun is less than about 32 degrees above the horizon. When the Sun is at 32 degrees, the arc appears as a patch, but as the sun lowers, the patch opens into an arc of color."

Light and water are a magical combination. The white light from the sun has locked in it the whole spectrum of colors which water, in the form of mist or droplets or ice crystals, can unlock and reveal. They spread in the sky like a fabulous bird fanning its tail. I think it's time to give the "circumzenith arc" (*Webster's* calls it a "circumzenithal arc"—a more attractive name. I suggest "sunbird." It flies much higher than the sundogs.

a red balloon
rises out of the park trees
into the blue sky

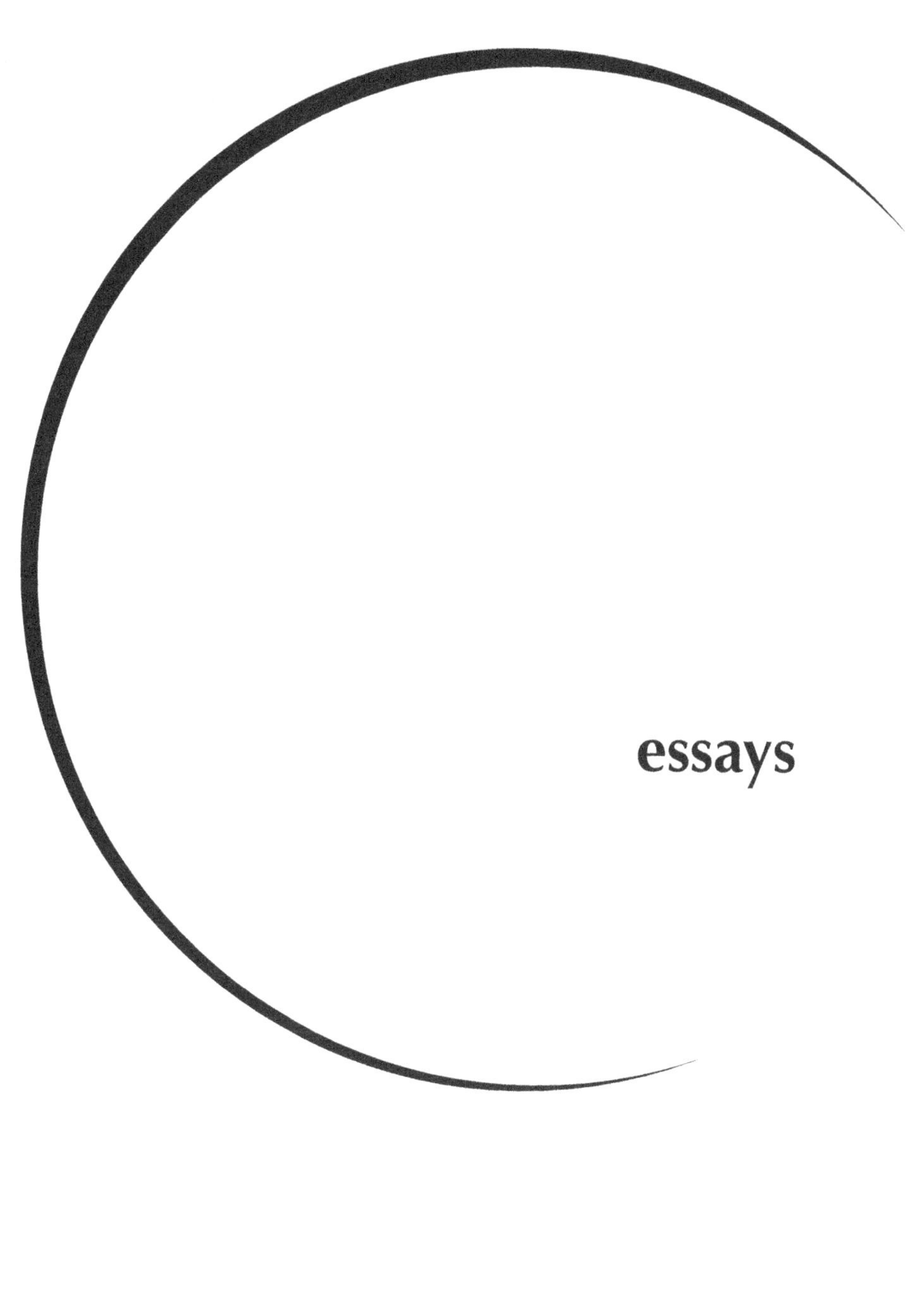

essays

Dee Evetts ✧ United States

The Conscious Eye: Divorce I

This past summer an old friend took issue with my commentary (in *Frogpond* XXIV.2) on Jane Reichhold's poem

> Mother's Day
> the daughter's call
> about her divorce[1]

I had read this as the daughter being caught up in her current problems, which are eclipsing the day's customary significance. My friend remarked that, as a woman, she must disagree with this interpretation. Unfortunately I never learned what her own take had been. My guess is that for her the poem was about solidarity between mother and daughter.

That is certainly one possibility—and no doubt there are still others. However, I question whether a reader's gender *per se* determines one's response to a piece of writing. I believe it is far more likely to be a reflection of our personal history and family relationships, and, to and extent, our convictions and ideals.

A more fundamental question is this: if we were to ask the poet what he or she intended, would the reply necessarily prove one reader wrong, and the other right? Surely that would impose an excessively narrow definition of "meaning." I would argue that a poem such as that above is to be regarded as richly ambiguous, appealing to different readers in different ways.

In a recent letter, Alice Frampton wrote, "I guess eventually you'll have to handle the kid stuff." Duly prompted, I have been looking at a half-dozen poems relating to custody and access, including this one of hers:

> between mom and dad
> the clickity-clack
> of suitcase wheels[2]

This can be placed alongside Tom Painting's

> my toddler
> helps pack her travel bag
> co-custody[3]

Both these poems, which depict similar scenes, remind us how the children of a divorce often have to grow up more quickly than their contemporaries. How desirable this is—how advantageous or harmful in the long term—is debatable, with so many other factors to be considered. My own parents divorced when I was nine, and for a few years I became to some degree my mother's companion and confidante. A child psychiatrist might frown over this; I recall thriving on it.

Frampton's poem is the more complex of these two, with her "clickity-clack" evoking a child's busy—even

fussy—concentration on a new skill. And there is a
nicely understated play on "between," which works
on both the spatial and relationship level. If there is
a price for this subtlety it is that the piece, if read on
its own without any supporting context, could give a
different picture altogether—that of a family going
off happily on vacation together.

Painting takes a simpler—almost naive—approach,
and what his poem depicts is unmistakable. One could
add, unremarkable. Yet the poet succeeds in making
his scene genuinely touching, rather than sentimental.

All of this prompts me to consider how we can
appreciate some haiku for their transparency, and
other because they are more opaque. On the one hand
Roberta Beary gives us a straightforward observation
of body language:

> custody hearing
> seeing his arms cross
> i uncross mine[4]

The message is clear, we appreciate the moment, end
of poem. Yet the same poet can challenger her readers
with

> court-ordered visit
> i take up her unfinished
> crossword[5]

There are deep currents here. While "unfinished" is
the crucial word (and we understand that it applies
to far more than just the crossword) there is also a
suggestion that the writer sees herself as holding on

to her daughter, by appropriating the puzzle she has put aside. Here is a haiku that, in its way, achieves the density of a psychological novel.

The more open-faced poems by their nature tend to have the most immediate impact. They may depend for their effect on a surprising turn or twist, typically in the last line. An example of this is found in John Stevenson's

> Christmas Day
>   the exchange
>   of custody[6]

Using just six words, and with a gentle yet rueful irony, the poet conveys how profoundly the holiday season has changed for this family.

Stevenson's poem can be contrasted with this by Claire Gallagher:

> weekend custody —
> granite boulders grow
> from remaining snow[7]

What is the significance of the disappearing now and the reappearing rocks? How do they relate to weekend custody? I feel that it all hangs together, without quite being able to say why. If pushed, I would venture the notion that the natural phenomena are providing this parent with a measure of time's passing, during this all-too-short weekend. We might also reflect that the children too are inexorably growing: nothing remains fixed or given.

But none of this serves as an adequate explanation.

As Edward Hirsch remarks in his lucid and passionate book How to Read a Poem: "The poem is an act beyond paraphrase, because what is said is always inseparable from the way it is being said." Gallagher's wonderfully elusive haiku serves as an apt illustration.

For purely circumstantial reasons, her poem recalls one of my own written a few years ago:

> custody battle
> a bodyguard lifts the child
> to see the snow[8]

I leave this picture with readers, to interpret as they please.

---

1. *A Dictionary of Haiku* (AHA Books 1992)
2. unpublished
3. *Brussels Sprout* XXII.2
4. *pocket change* (towpath anthology, Red Moon Press 2000)
5. unpublished
6. *Red Moon Anthology* 1996
7. *Frogpond* XXI.3
8. *endgrain* (Red Moon Press 1997)

Dee Evetts   ✧   United States

The Conscious Eye: Divorce II

This series, given the volume and quality of work available, could easily have continued to document the experience of divorce for several more issues. Nevertheless I have decided to conclude it by focusing on a particular aspect: the spectrum of possible relationships involving ex-spouses and new partners.

Some years ago a writer friend of mine gave a birthday party. Among the people she invited were here ex-husband, her partner of ten years who succeeded him, and her current lover. I anticipated an awkward occasion, but was proved wrong. The three men sat together consuming large quantities of cake and swapping anecdotes about my friend's eccentric mother in California.

I am inclined to treasure this as some kind of ideal in human behavior. Yet who knows in fact what hidden currents were coursing through even that convivial scene? The following poem by Stacy Pendergrast explores a not dissimilar situation:

> my ex's wife
> serves me cherry pie
> on our old chipped china[1]

This evokes a range of conflicting emotions while

the connotations of "cherry" (on the one hand erotic, on the other recalling the old song, "Can She Bake a Cherry Pie?") seem to threaten the containment — the effort by both women to be "civilized."

Tony Pupello does something comparable in the domestic arena with his

    family reunion:
    his ex squeezes
    fresh lemonade[2]

Here the play on "squeezes" is quite overt, which makes it at first glance a less complex and at the same time more humorous piece. Then I wonder: isn't "fresh lemonade" as suggestive as anything in the preceding poem? In any case, both poets deftly exploit the perennial entanglement of food and love.

The poems remaining for discussion are so diverse that I am going to present them, somewhat capriciously, in what might be their chronological order. By this I mean: along the timeline of months or years following the break-up in each case. Readers may disagree stridently with my placings, but that after all is half the fun.

    the stillness
    when I call him
    by my ex's name[3]

We may hope that this is early in the course of events, for the more time has elapsed the more resounding that stillness is likely to be. Nancy Young lets us overhear one of those irretrievable slips of the tongue, so understandable and so human, which can severely shake a new relationship — if not derail it.

> Father's Day
> she tells me
> I'm not the father[4]

It is anyone's guess where this, by John Stevenson, belongs. It could be years before, or years after the separation — or anywhere in between. Regardless, what impresses me is that while it reports a callous, perhaps even deliberately cruel outburst, there is no trace of complaint or recrimination in the poem. At most, a shocked silence.

> no longer married
> only their shadows touch
> . . . graduation day[5]

A few years on, seems to be about right for Roberta Beary's chilly rendition of estrangement. It is hard to imagine the former couple getting even this close together, unless compelled by circumstances.

Perhaps parallel in the time-frame, yet as far removed as can be, is the enduring connection implied by Michael Cross:

> winter afternoon —
> filling the half-flat tire
> for my ex-wife[6]

Is there any other way to read this than as an understated yet unqualified testament to the transforming power of tenderness? Probably there is, but just now I don't want to hear about it. (A footnote to these two poems: the bleak one is set in summer, the warm one in winter. Each gains from the contrast.)

> still and all
> news of my ex's divorce
> unsettles me[7]

Generally speaking this kind of statement makes for weak haiku. But Charles Trumbull retrieves everything with a middle line that conjures a vivid moment (a telephone call, a letter in hand, a conversation overheard—we supply the picture) leaving himself with two lines for conveying its effect. And this remains ambiguous, in a way that feels completely authentic. Is the poet unsettled because of concern for his ex-wife? Because he may have to fill some new role? Or because she has in some sense become available again? Possibly all of the above, or each in turn.

> Divorced years ago . . .
> but the pine that we planted
> towers over her yard[8]

Even if Tom Tico had not confirmed this, I would have reckoned at least two decades of history here. The poem offers us no explicit feeling, yet there is an underlying sense of wonder and consolation. It is conceivable that the speaker is merely passing by his former wife's home. Equally believable, that he has known the shade of that tree, and in her company. Ultimately which picture we choose will reflect our own experiences and ideals.

I wish to thank all the poets who have contributed to this series, including those I have been unable to feature. I believe that most would testify to the cathartic and healing power of such work, both as writers and as readers. Certainly this has been true in my own case, and I am grateful for it.

------

1. unpublished
2. *Acorn* 4
3. *Black Bough* 13
4. *Modern Haiku* XXX.3
5. *A New Resonance* 2 (Red Moon Press 2001)
6. *ibid.*
7. *Modern Haiku* XXIX.2
8. *Spring Morning Sun* (Belltower Press 1998)

Dee Evetts ✧ United States

The Conscious Eye: 9/11

It was inevitable that poets around the world would feel compelled to write about the events of September 11, 2001. And haiku poets were certainly no exception to this. About a month after the attacks I began collecting material for an article in this series, intending it to be published for the first anniversary of the disaster.

I have in the process looked at hundreds of poems, and what strikes me first is the sincerity and depth of feeling expressed in so many different ways. However, my second observation has to be that the great majority are artistically weak. There is no doubt that the writing of them was cathartic, and that is important in itself. But good poetry is on another plane from good therapy. It must aspire to be an utterance that transcends the particulars while remaining rooted in them. At best it will be timeless, despite having its genesis in a very specific time.

Graphic depictions and patriotic declarations (two broad headings under which very many poems fell) are unlikely to reach this level of expression It may take a very experienced poet indeed, and we have on in Cor van den Heuvel. Below are two of the several haiku he wrote after 9/11:

looking south
the stain on the sky
day after day[1]

at the bar
my first ballgame since the attack
blue sky[2]

These are intimate poems, and that is the basis of their strength. Countless readers, today as well as in years to come, will identify with these experiences. Thus may a single voice acquire universal significance.

More specifically, in the first poem we understand that the stain on the sky—the column of smoke that dominated Lower Manhattan for weeks—can also be seen as a stain on humanity. In the second poem the contrasting impulses—to mourn, and to affirm the persistence of life—are conveyed by an otherwise commonplace bar scene, rendered singular by the poet's response to a clear sky above the televised ballpark.

Closer still to Ground Zero, in Tony Pupello's

after the bombing
in the fine ash
pigeon tracks[3]

the poet is less visible. Nonetheless this too has the feel of immediate experience, offering an acute observation that locates the global within the personal.

It might be argued that these two poets had the advantage (if such a term can apply in this context) of being New Yorkers, who witnessed these momentous events at close quarters. My reply would be that they used the material to hand—and skillfully. At a greater distance Tom Painting was equally effective, focusing on that which touched his own life, and by extension, all others:

> as our kids
> sift the beach sand
> reconnaissance flights[4]

By contrast, the many attempts by haiku poets across the country to represent the scenes in New York and Washington D.C. (though understandable enough, given the massive television coverage) were largely misdirected. Caroline Banks proved to be one of the exceptions, surprising us with irony:

> 9/11 migration
> wondering what else
> the geese know[5]

> more anthrax
> eating all the chocolate
> from our survival cache[6]

That these poems come so close to being humorous could make some readers uneasy. I find them honest, and a refreshingly truthful examination of human responses to danger. (One might also ask: if we forget how to smile, then what is survival for?)

Predictably enough, the American flag appears with great frequency in haiku about 9/11 and its aftermath. Regrettably few poets managed to go beyond some version of simple flag-waving. Two who adopted a more thoughtful approach were Charlie Trumbull and Judson Evans:

> tangled in the neighbor's
> Halloween cobwebs
> his American flag[7]

> after five months
> seeing through
> the overpass flag[8]

Both of these poems are firmly grounded in a literal level of meaning, with a phrasing that then suggests a great deal more. The key word in Trumbull's poem is "tangled," prompting us to consider just how confused our patriotism can become—how it gets caught up in so much else.

The play on "seeing through" in Evans' poem is quite masterly. As I understand it, what the poet sees through in the larger sense is what any national flag ultimately represents: the naive and dangerous myth of a virtuous "us" and an evil "them."

With the passing of time, haiku have naturally appeared that have an elegiac quality. I particularly like this one by an'ya:

> the passing year
> a jetliner disappears
> into gray clouds[9]

There is a sense of innocence lost (we will never again watch a jetliner slide into a cloud with eyes entirely free of past horror) yet at the same time, of normality reasserted.

A more traditional approach is taken by Yasuhiko Shigemoto:

> on the site
> of the World Trade Center
> summer grasses[10]

Although the last line is a common enough season word, its use in this context leads me to assume that the poet intends a reference to Bashō's famous

> Summer grass—
> all that's left
> of warrior's dreams.
> (translation Robert Hass)

This is an apt connection to make, enlarging our frame of reference and reminding us the more effectively that all things must pass, and equally that there will be regeneration of a kind.

---

1. *Haikukai* No. 61, December 2002
2. *ibid.*
3. unpublished
4. unpublished
5. unpublished
6. unpublished
7. *South by Southeast* 9.1
8. unpublished
9. *The Heron's Nest* IV.1
10. unpublished

Jim Kacian ✧ United States
John Stevenson ✧ United States

Haiku Readings

Each issue of *Frogpond* contains 100-140 haiku and senryū. Some of these go on to have further lives by being anthologized or included in individual collections, singled out for analysis in a "Favorite Haiku" piece, or perhaps even winning an award. Still, it seems as though these poems are too fleetingly in our consciousness. In light of this we offer some comment on work which appeared in *Frogpond* XXV.2, and welcome your brief comments on what you may have appreciated about poems appearing in the current issue.

> too hot to sleep . . .
> from the fire truck's siren
> a map of the streets
> *Dave Russo*

Some of us consider summer our least favorite season. Some of us can strongly identify with the struggle to leave the day behind and enter the relative comfort of sleep. And for us, too, the failed effort to sleep on such nights often manifests itself as near-hallucinatory thoughts, imbued with an obsession for ordering, counting, categorizing, or, as in this case, mapping. While we may have suspected that others had these experiences or something like them, we may also have felt alone in this. Here is a moment of confirmation and, with that, a moment of comfort, which beautifully counterbalances the discomfort and disorientation of the original image.

We like the fact that humidity is not mentioned in the poem. For us, this makes it the air of the poem, the invisible element which is present everywhere.

And, we like the fact that this is the sort of poem that might have been written directly from experience. In other words, the author may have given up on sleeping, turned the light on and written this down. Whether it came that immediately for Dave Russo is unimportant. But the fact that it feels that immediate adds greatly to its appeal for us.

> Spring too,
> in ancient times;
> snow on the mosaic
>> *Erica Facey*

Within the brief compass of a single haiku we rarely have the luxury of time travel, and when we do, it's usually something in the present which makes us reminisce. This unusual poem not only takes us centuries into the past, but returns us to the present in the same instant. We can't know exactly the theme of the mosaic, but we can surmise that it provides the same inspiration to the poet as it did to the artist so long ago, and was bound up with the eternal cycling of the seasons.

surprised by which
handbag she likes
mid-summer night
    Michael Fessler

And ancient wisdom bound up in modern guise: midsummer night is the night of mutability, the night of the longest day, the feast of the Heras, those women in full communion with the mysteries of the Great Goddess. It is fitting that the poet, a male, be surprised by even the most casual choice of a woman on this day, and that while he notes it, it is really nothing out of the ordinary, either.

a path of leaves
our conversation
turns wordless
    Christopher Patchel

It is an old truism that some people become such great friends that they can dispense with words. Whether that is the normal state for these conversers or not, they arrive at such a point during the course of this precisely articulated poem. The path of leaves does not mark and end to conversation, but to a different mode of it. The eloquence shifts from the human to the elemental, and the fallen leaves are the aural accompaniment to the continuing, unheard dialogue.

evening Mass
my father's voice
beside me
    Cindy Guentherman

There are three fathers in this compact poem: the father (priest) conducting the mass, "our father who art in heaven," and "my father" who is "beside me" and has a voice we can hear with ease.

Peggy Willis Lyles ✧ United States

Black and White

family album—
the black and white
of my youth
Jim Kacian

Nature has its seasons, and so do our human lives. Focusing on a family album, Jim Kacian experiences a moment of heightened awareness and insight that links his personal life to a particular time and place in cultural and social history.

Technology has changed. Color photography is the norm now and has been for some time. The black and white family pictures from his youth are dated in more ways than one. What was once commonplace and expected seems odd, catching the author's attention and adding to the sense of transience the pictures must already have stirred. I think of my own family photographs, black and white, sometimes glossy, sometimes matte, right through the fifties, with color snapshots becoming more prevalent from the mid-sixties onward.

A far more profound change was taking place in the United States during those same years. Race was a major issue as society slowly and painfully moved toward integration. Jim Kacian was born in 1953. In

Brown v. Board of Education of Topeka, May 17, 1954, the Supreme Court ruled that compulsory segregation in public schools denied equal protection under the law. In 1955 Rosa Parks was jailed for refusing to give up her bus seat to a white passenger. The successful bus boycott soon followed, as did the Civil Rights Act of 1957. By the time Kacian was old enough to be aware of such things, the Civil Rights Movement was well underway. Growing up in the Sixties, he witnessed a decade of struggle and reform that revolutionized society. Whatever his family album may or may not show of the upheaval, the mature poet is surely conscious of it as he looks back and thinks of "black and white."

Chances are he also thinks of the black and white of oversimplification. Often the young are passionate, seeing right and wrong as clear opposites. The elders of any generation may become "set in their ways," adhering to fixed codes, regardless of how well those codes stand up to tests of logic. While practically all established standards of behavior came into question during the Sixties, the moral judgments of that era seem simple and innocent compared to those of later decades.

Kacian's poem is compressed, seemingly artless, and infused with expansive energy. It appeals to the senses, the emotions, and the intellect. Ordinary language and readily available associations open large spaces for the reader to enter and explore. Just nine words link to a whole era and speak clearly of transience and awesome change. The last line brings us back to the personal, and the poem circles to its beginning. The family album is a concrete and meaningful presence. The poet's tone is somewhat detached and slightly humorous as he focuses on the black and white photographs, intuitively recognizing all those shades of gray.

Emiko Miyashita ✧ Japan

Kukai: Its Purpose and Effects

Haiku is a literature of ordinary people. It can be refined through practice and training with the help of other haiku friends. A *kukai* functions as the training system.

Mrs. Yoshiko Yoshino, the master of *Hoshi* (*Star*) Haiku Group in Japan, says that a *kukai* is the place to bring up the students. Her selections are based on two standards: choosing perfect haiku for her special selections; and regular selections for particular haiku that will encourage the students toward higher goals. As a haiku master, Mrs. Yoshino can tell which haiku is written by whom. She chooses haiku that reflect the individuality of each student, without regard to its degree of achievement in style, grammar, or haiku skills. Therefore we may define *kukai* as the training gymnasium for these skills.

In Japan, most haiku poets belong to a haiku group led by such a master. I belong to the *Ten'i* (*Providence*) haiku group, led by Dr. Akito Arima. The haiku we bring to the *kukai* are passed around anonymously and are selected by both the master and the members. Each haiku selected is "born" as a haiku and is printed in the *kukaiho*, the record of the *kukai*. Each haiku group publishes a haiku journal, and the haiku selected by the master each month are printed in it.

The advantage of the *kukai* system is that one will know immediately whether or not one's haiku is deemed acceptable. At the same time, we know which haiku have attracted the attention or support from *kukai* members. Thus we can learn which poems are good and which are not so good; and whether we used language successfully. In addition appropriate examples of good *kigo* teach us to use *kigo* effectively. Within a *kukai* poets are invited to worlds one can never visit when writing haiku at a desk alone.

In Japan, we are asked how many years we have been practicing haiku. Ten years of practice is still considered an amateur level. This is my ninth year of practicing haiku and therefore I am still a haiku infant in Japan! Dr. Arima has been writing haiku for 56 years and Masajo Suzuki, the author of *Love Haiku*, for more than 64 years. Mrs. Yoshino, the author of *Tsuru*, for almost 60 years! The longer the better, we believe. There is an additional system called the *dojin* system; *dojin* means "leading member." Those who write good haiku are given a title of *dojin* from the master. When one receives this title one is permitted to teach haiku to other people. I received the *dojin* title in 1999 in my sixth years of haiku practice.

What I would like to emphasize here is that attending a *kukai* and learning from it is the key to becoming a good haiku poet in the Japanese haiku pond. The haiku we bring to the *kukai*, usually three to five, do not represent our entire personality, but only a bit of our poetic essence. If they are not accepted or selected, we get an opportunity to think about why they were not selected: how is it flawed? is it a weak poem? When we encounter a haiku with the same theme as ours presented in a more sophisticated or polished way, we simply give out a sigh of admiration, *ah!* and learn. The feeling of rejection is the last reaction haiku poets should take—one's attitude should be positive throughout the process of *kukai* and after. We do learn a lot from *kukai*, by selecting, by being selected and by not being selected.

The points of selecting haiku in our *kukai* in the Japanese haiku pond are:

> whether it is written in haiku form of 5-7-5 Japanese *moji*
> whether it has a *kigo*, and a *kire* (a break for pause or juxtaposition) and the *kire* occurs only once
> whether the *kigo* in the haiku is working effectively
> whether it recreates the image in the reader's mind accurately
> whether the economizing of words is done effectively—unnecessary adjectives and adverbs are checked; not more than one verb in a haiku is preferred
> whether the haiku has not become mere explanation
> whether it is focused sharply to what the poet wants to say
> whether it is not a copy of some other haiku that was written in the past
> whether the haiku is not said fully—we leave room for the reader to complete it
> whether the haiku reads well in a fine rhythm
> whether or not you like it!

We encourage people to win all the games in which they participate. However, I think we can learn more when we fail. A *kukai* is usually held every month, so we do have a chance each month to try again to make people say *Ah!* to our haiku. What a challenge and what an excitement to be blessed with *kukai* colleagues who can provide such a good training!

Mrs. Yoshino has been the master of the International Haiku Salon in Matsuyama for many years. When she makes comment on foreigner's haiku in English, she pays full respect to their cultural background and will never impose rules applied for haiku written in Japanese. She says she prefers to have the English haiku written in three lines, the middle line slightly longer than the rest. She has noticed that English haiku contain more explanatory words and phrases. For example, when writing about a piece of cloud, it is likely that the English haiku use a descriptive word like fluffy, single thread of, white or purple, etc. to explain what kind of cloud it is. Or when the haiku already contains a word indicating autumn, such as "crickets," the poem uses an unnecessary word indicating the season, such as "autumn" before the cloud. It is best if the reader can picture his/her own kind of cloud by reading the haiku. And in a good haiku, after reading the whole haiku, the kind of the cloud can be defined automatically. Mrs. Yoshino thinks that these explanations are not necessary in haiku. But these observations come from her Japanese haiku tradition. For haiku poets who write in languages other than Japanese, she thinks it is important for each poet to write in his/her mosst comfortable way. Therefore these Japanese haiku rules may not be automatically applied to judge or appreciate the English language haiku.

H. F. Noyes ✧ Greece

A Favorite Haiku

wild roses
tarrying beside one
touched by time
Robert Spiess

The poet lingers by a fading wild rose long enough to feel empathy. In Isaiah it is said that "we all do fade as a leaf." This haiku is a fine example of *aware*, which Alan Watts characterizes as "not quite grief, not quite nostalgia." It has the right tone to perfection. One feels nature's way is accepted, without sorrow or regret.

Bruce Ross   ✧   United States

Notes from the Prairie

Sueko Sameshima, who neither speaks nor writes English, was born in British Columbia in 1915 but received his elementary and junior high school education in Japan. He moved around western Canada for many years and was placed in a relocation camp in southern Alberta during World War II. Most of his life has been subsequently spent among the prairies of southern Alberta, and his haiku, consistently published in Canada and Japan, often reflect the starkness of those landscapes.

BR: When did you first learn haiku and what did you think about the haiku you first read?

SS: In the beginning of the spring of 1940, I ran into my friend who took me to a meeting of the Kamome Haiku Group in Port Alberni, British Columbia. Since then, I have been involved with haiku.

BR: When did you write your first haiku and do you remember it?

SS: My initial haiku

haruno kaze typist shiroku kubi makaru

spring cold
the typist has a white scarf
around her neck

received a good evaluation, and since the I have been more interested in and have kept writing haiku.

BR: You were born in British Columbia, educated as a young man in Japan, and then finally settled in the prairies of southern Alberta. How has this moving around affected your haiku?

SS: In the beginning of 1940 I found myself at the Tashme Relocation Camp, so I found 30-40 members and established the Tashibi Haiku Group. I edited two volumes of concentration camp haiku journals until the camp dissolved.

BR: Were you part of the Japanese community that fled British Columbia during World War II to escape the internment camp? If so, how did this experience affect your relation to haiku?

SS: I look back at that time and wonder: Could this have been my most fulfilling experience with haiku?

BR: Haiku is a Japanese form of poetry. You have lived in Canada in the prairies of Alberta most of your life. How does Japanese haiku become different for someone living in the Canadian prairies?

SS: When the war ended, I started to look for a job. I went from place to place with different jobs at beet farms in Moossejaw, Saskatchewan, Winnipeg, Manitoba, and southern Alberta. I have settled in Coaldale for 50 years.

After I left the camp, I was exhausted and not able to find a job and many other things. Also, my haiku friends moved from British Columbia to Quebec. Even any kind of exchange with my haiku friends stopped. Therefore, there was a time I stopped writing haiku for almost 10 years.

When my life was settled, I could afford to start writing haiku again. I was enthused to send my haiku to Japan and continue writing haiku. I was attracted to the natural environment and the change of seasons in the prairies. Although the land seemed barren, I began to notice how the impressions of the landscape were deeply engraved into my heart.

BR: You have two especially powerful haiku collected in the Canadian Haiku Anthology, edited by Dorothy Howard and André Duhaime. One is

kasha sugite soredake no kei yukikoya

> a train passes
> and then the only view
> snowfield

The other is

katamaru mo hanarete tatsu mo iteru ushi

> the cows stand together
> and one stands by itself
> but all are freezing

Do you remember creating each of these? Can you say something about the circumstances and what you feel about the experiences you presented in these haiku?

SS: The prairie snowfield in the first haiku looks like the Pacific Ocean. Sometimes, a train passed silently and I could not see the steam because of the distance and the dark. And then, I would go back to view the snowfield. The snowfield is eternally captivating. As to the second haiku seven or eight cows were gathered and one cow stood separately in a field. Like an unmoving stick none of them seemed to move. I thought I was just looking at the cows. However, I realized that I was also standing, watching them like an unmoving stick.

BR: Can you say something about the pleasure haiku gives you?

SS: I really enjoy reading other people's haiku. I would be very happy if others understood my own haiku. I would hope to continue taking haiku walks just as many Japanese Canadians enjoy playing golf and other sports.

* * *

(Translations by Bruce Ross and Yuko Okui.)

fuyubare no koku ni tskamu chiri mo nashi

> in clear winter
> there is nothing in the sky
> not even dust

aomugino hatega chi no hate sumitsukishi

> young wheat
> up to the very end of the land
> remaining forever

ichizan no momiji kando fumamu kana

> on one of the mountains
> red maples leaves cover the path —
> should I step on them?

yukigekaze waga soshin no taza yurumu

> snow-melting wind
> all of my feelings in
> a bucket rope come loose

hyokako ni kurenai chirashi poppy muru

> frozen lake
> the falling crimson poppies
> gather together

ryokuin no karasu ga ah-ah-to oi yoberu

> in the shade of a tree
> a crow is cawing
> I feel old

chichi to ko no onaji heyanari nesho-gatsu

> father and child
> sleeping over in the same room
> New Year

Jianquing Zheng ✧ United States

Tangible Imagination in Richard Wright's Haiku

Haiku, a short poetic form, always challenges the reader to imagine and sense. Asataro Miyamori says that "an ideal haiku is one in which a natural event is described as it is, and the poet's emotion does not appear on the surface." Because of its brevity, haiku focuses on a momentary impression or, let me borrow Robert Frost's phrase, a momentary stay of confusion.

A good haiku with the qualities of brevity, ellipsis, and suggestiveness should have space for a reader to fill in his interpretation and aesthetic appreciation. Also, a haiku's images should produce a montage effect for the reader to associate nature with human ideas. Read this haiku by Richard Wright:

From a tenement,
The blue jazz of a trumpet
Weaving autumn mists. (#253)

This haiku produces a picture that interacts between visual and auditory images. The poet not only literally hears the sounds of a trumpet but sees it weaving autumn mists in his imagination as well. He also challenges the reader to appreciate it aesthetically based on the interaction of the senses. The intangible quality of atmosphere and mood created by Wright with tangible words reminds me of a classical Chinese quatrain "Deer Fence" written by Wang Wei, a Tang dynasty poet (701–761):

> In vast mountains I see no one
> But hear human voices echoing.
> Sunset rays into deep woods
> And shines again on green moss.

Wang Wei's "Deer Fence" also invites the reader's imagination with the interaction of visual and auditory images. A visitor sees no one around but hears the echo of human voices. There is peace hanging over there in the mountains, especially when the setting sun casts back its rays through the deep woods and shines again on the green moss. Here is another haiku by Wright:

> From across the lake,
> Past the black winter trees,
> Faint sounds of a flute. (#571)

What does Wright want us to imagine in this haiku? What is the connection between nature (the visual images of lake, black winter trees) and sounds of a flute? What does the flute symbolize? To understand the haiku, first draw a sketch in your mind: someone is playing the flute and its sound reaches across the lake where someone else is listening. This auditory image of the sound of a flute joins artfully the visual images of lake, blackness, winter, and trees. In fact, both the auditory and the visual images intensify each other. The flute symbolizes art created by humans and its joining with those visual images implies an interrelationship with nature. It invites human involvement so that the poet listens and observes attentively on the other side of the lake. In other words, he enjoys art aesthetically. This terse, elliptic, and suggestive haiku creates a momentary impression through the visual and auditory images. It is a beautiful, evocative haiku.

WORKS CITED

Miyamori, Asataro. *An Anthology of Haiku: Ancient and Modern*. Westport: Greenwood, 1970.

Wright, Richard. *Haiku: This Other World*. New York: Arcade, 1998.

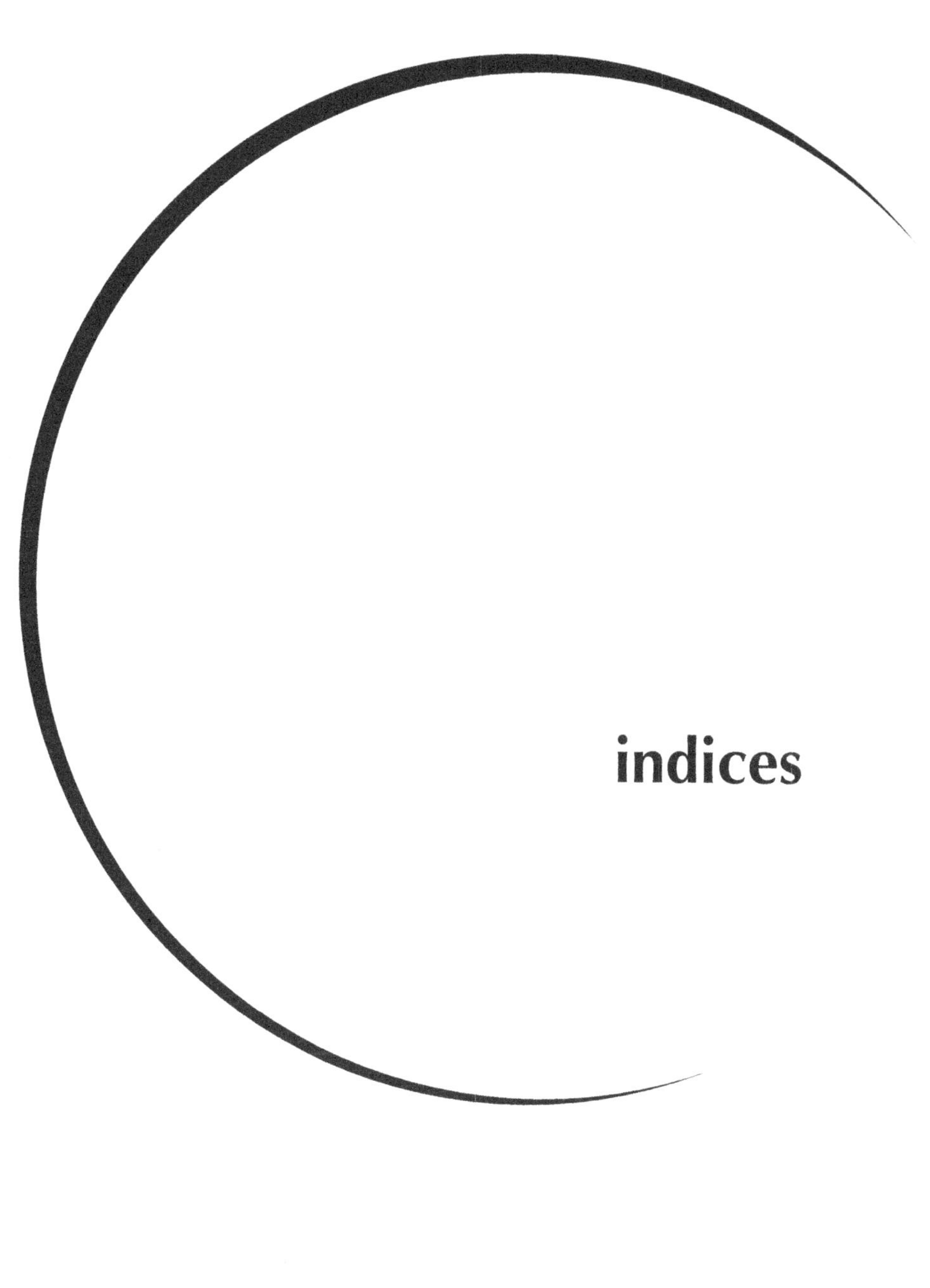

indices

index of authors

acknowledgments

Andreescu—"nursing home" *RAW NerVZ* VIII.1; **Atkinson**—"on the memorial" *Time Haiku* 15; **Avis**—"the dada exhibit" *RAW NerVZ* VIII.1; **Babusci**—"snow-covered village" *Frogpond* XXV.2; **Banwarth**—"first night of snow" Drevniok 2002; **Baranski**—"Prison lights out" *Convicts Shoot the Breeze*; **Barlow**—"skinning squid" *Flamingo Shapes*; **Barry**—"strangers' voices" *Time Haiku* 15; **Barwell**—"reverie" *Presence* 18; **Beary**—"third date" Penumbra Contest 2002; **Berry**—"doorbell" *Paper Wasp* 8.3, "desert heat" HPNC2002; **Board**—"not showiing up" *Frogpond* XXV.3; **Bose**—"deep in the woods" *Mayfly* 32; **Bostian**—"arguing in bed" *Frogpond* XXV.1; **Brooks, M.**—"autumn mist" *snapshots* 9; **Brooks, R.**—"25th anniversary" *RAW NerVZ* VII.3; **Brydges-Jones**—"monday" *Presence* 18; **Bullock**—"ex-junkie" *Frogpond* XXV.3; **Cabalona**—"Deep winter" *Frogpond* XXV.3; **Chang**—"end of the walk" "happy hour" *Upstate Dim Sum* 3; **Clausen**—"turning it down" *Frogpond* XXV.3; **Cobb**—"spring break-up" *RAW NerVZ* VIII.1; **Compton**—"winter storm watch" *Modern Haiku* XXXIII.3; **crook**—"fifth birthday" *Still* 5.3; **Cullen**—"first snow" *bottle rockets* 7.1; **Dahl**—"old garden shed" Kusamakura 2001; **Delaney**—"sipping champagne" *bottle rockets* 7.1; **Deming**—"shifting" *Frogpond* XXV.2; **Deodhar**—"haiga workshop" *Presence* 2002; **Detheridge**—"quiet enough" *Blithe Spirit* 11.4; **Devidé**—"New Year's Day" *Woodpecker* 8.2; **Dolphy**—"temple rockpool" *Presence* 16; **Doughty**—"Haibun" *Frogpond* XXV.1; **Dunphy**—"war crimes trial" *Frogpond* XXV.1; "Battered Customers" *RAW NerVZ* VII.4; **Elliott**—"January storm" *Haiku International Anthology*; **Epstein**—"Each swig" *Frogpond* XXV.1; **Evans, J.**—"The Word for It" *summer dreams*; **Evans, M.**—"Agate Beach" HPNC2001; **Evetts**—"recycling day" *Frogpond* XXV.1, "The Conscious Eye—Divorce I" *Frogpond* XXV.1, "The Conscious Eye—Divorce II" *Frogpond* XXV.2, "The Conscious Eye—9/11" *Frogpond* XXV.3; **Farid**—"Boxing Day" *Blithe Spirit* XII.1; **Figgins**—"empty kitchen" *South by Southeast* 9.2; **Fixter**—"talking in his sleep" *Blithe Spirit* XII.1; **Ford**—"a cold wind blows" *Haiku Canada Newsletter* XV.2; **Forrester**—"cereal box" *snapshots* 9; **Fraticelli**—"seniors' residence" *Haiku Canada Newsletter* XV.3; **Gallagher**—"after love" Drevniok 2002, "nine-month belly" *The Heron's Nest* IV.2; **Gay**—"Floating mist" *Presence* 2001; **Gershator**—"on hold" *Frogpond* XXV.2; **Gibbons**—"farmyard track" *Blithe Spirit* XII.1; **Gilli**—"first azaleas" *Acorn* 8; **Gieske-Pieters**—"one by one" *Woodpecker* 8.2; **Goldring**—"january thaw" *Haiku Canada Newsletter* XV.3; **Gorman**—"all day rain" *Modern Haiku* XXXIII.3; **Grimnes**—"first snow" *South by Southeast* 9.3; **Gurga**—"summer harbor" *Haiku International Anthology*; **Hall**—"smiling through tears" *RAW NerVZ* VII.4, "Hanging on Every Word" HPNC Rengay 2001, "Pop Goes the Weasel" *Mariposa* 6; **Hardenbrook**—"solstice afternoon" *haijinx* 2.1; **Harpeng**—"twilight drizzle" *Mayfly* 32; **Hazen**—"Shadows Cross" *Modern Haiku* XXXIII.3; **Herold**—"Mt. St. Helens" *haijinx* 2.1; **Hill**—"midnight lightning" *Presence* 18; **Hotham**—"a late arrival" Kusamakura 2001, "no name for his illness" *The Heron's Nest* IV.7, "the sun's warmth" *The Heron's Nest* IV.9; **houck**—"the same old tom" *RAW NerVZ* VII.4; **Howard**—"hum of the wheel" *Modern Haiku* XXXIII.2; **Johnson**—"cycling" *Frogpond* XXV.3; **Jones**—"Three Minute Silence" *Blithe Spirit* 11.4, "The Spirit Level" *summer dreams*; **Kacian**—"cemetery" *ant* 5, "three-quarter moon" *mariposa* 6, "a letter from a prisoner" *snapshots* 9, "Eastertide" *summer dreams*, "beneath a waxing moon" *Modern Haiku* XXXIII.3, "Haiku Readings" *Frogpond* XXV.3; **Karkow**—"alone again" Drevniok 2002, "Cheek to Cheek" HPNC Rengay 2001; **Ketchek**—"windstorm" *bottle rockets* 7; **Kettner**—"your hair drawn back" *ant* 5; **Klontz**—"country road" *snapshots* 9; **Kurnik**—"forest path" Kaji Aso 2002; **Laliberte-Carey**—"rising moon" *Acorn* 8, "baggage claim" *Frogpond* XXV.1, "jeavy traffic" *haijinx* 2.1; **Lausé**—"after the rain" *Frogpond* XXV.2; **Lavery**—"wrong number" *Presence* 17; **Leuck**—"after winter" *Haiku Canada Newsletter* XV.2; **Lofvers**—"Haibun" *Woodpecker* 8.1; **Lucas**—"the echo behind" *Blithe Spirit* 12.1; **Lyles**—"Black and White" *The Heron's Nest* IV.9; **m.**—"back again" *Acorn* 8; **Machmiller**—"the remaining snow" *Blush of Winter Moon*; **Makiko**—"flea market" *Frogpond* XXV.3; **Malito**—"late May sun" *Haiku Canada Newsletter* XV.3, "midweek rain" *Acorn* 8; **Markowski**—"Charity Ball" *Modern Haiku* XXXIII.3; **Mason**—"prison wall" *Blithe Spirit* 12.1; **Matsumoto**—"knowing your cough" *Frogpond* XXV.1; **McClintock**—"walking home" *Still* 5.3, "Gangaa-mahaa-nadii" *summer dreams*, "Unnatural Amber" *Frogpond* XXV.3, "The Lotus Eaters" *Frogpond* XXV.2; **McLaughlin**—"husband and wife" *Modern Haiku* XXXIII.1; **Mena**—"hot summer night" *Still* 5.3; **Mill**—"evensong" *haijinx* 2.1; **Missias**—"summer evening" *Frogpond* XXV.2; **Miyashita**—"Kuikai" *Frogpond* XXV.2; **Morden**—"first day of spring" *Haiku Canada Newsletter* XV.3; **Naia**—"tumbling snowflakes" *Frogpond* XXV.2; **Ness**—"shifting clouds" *RAW NerVZ* VIII.1, "another hot day" *Haiku Canada Newsletter* XV.3, "in remission" *Haiku Canada Newsletter* XV.2; **Neilsen**—"a single man's thoughts" *Acorn* 8; **Noyes**—"subway poster" *RAW NerVZ* VII.4, "A Favorite Haiku" *Modern Haiku* XXXIII.3; **Olson**—"with just enough" *Mayfly* 32, "witherred" *Frogpond* XXV.2; **Otaka**—"A firefly" *Haiku International Anthology*; **owen**—"bare trees" *Acorn* 8, "day's end" *bottle rockets* 7, "Canoe" & "September Rain" *Frogpond* XXV.2; **Painting**—"password" *South by Southwest* 9.3, "spring plowing" *Frogpond* XXV.2; **Patchel**—"tall grass" *haijinx* 2.1; **piper**—"wishing fountain" *Frogpond* XXV.1; **Pupello**—"talk of separation" *RAW NerVZ* VIII.1; **Ramesh**—"a yellow leaf" HPNC Rengay 2001; **Robeck**—"For Sale sign" *snapshots* 9, "menstruation" *Frogpond* XXV.1; **Rohrig**—"Hanging on Every Word" *Frogpond* XXIII:1, "Pop Goes the Weasel" *mariposa* 6, "In another life" & "Bird on the Wing" *Haiku Canada Newsletter* XV.2, "Ash Wednesday" *Frogpond* XXV.3; **Romano**—"death watch" *Frogpond* XXV.2; **Rosenstock**—"Cry of seagulls" *International Haiku Anthology*; **Ross**—"spring morning" *Frogpond* XXV.3, "Notes from the Prairie" *Frogpond* XXV.2; **Rossiter**—"bordertown motel" *Modern Haiku* XXXIII.3; **Rowland**—"the table" flat; **Russell**—"zen garden" Kaji Aso 2002; **Rutter**—"mad again" *Frogpond* XXV.2; **Saracevic**—"sharpening the ax" *Woodpecker* 8.2; **Sari**—"school graffiti" *Paper Wasp* 8.2; **Savage**—"psych ward" *Beyond Spring Rain*, "light in the wings" *RAW NerVZ* VIII.1; **Scott**—"icemelt" *Presence* 16; **Shigemoto**—"the sunset glow" *Haiku International Anthology*; **Shimield**—"Up escalator" *Blithe Spirit* 11.4; **Smith**—"winter solitude" *starfish* 6; **Spiess**—"an old folks home" *Mayfly* 32; **Spurgeon**—"new boots" *Modern Haiku* XXXIII.3; **St Jacques**—"home from hospital" *haijinx* 2.1; **Steel**—"Easter morning" *Acorn* 8; **Steele**—"stuck to the slab" *Blithe Spirit* 11.4; **Stefanac**—"because he asked" *RAW NerVZ* VII.4; **Steinberg**—"Scotch Neat" *Frogpond* XXV.2; **Stevenson**—"fireworks" *The Heron's Nest* IV.1, "applauding" *Upstate Dim Sum* II.1, "jampacked" *Frogpond* XXV.2, "Haiku Readings" *Frogpond* XXV.3; **Steyn**—"Cheek to Cheek" HPNC Rengay 2001; **Swede**—"airport lounge" *Modern Haiku* XXXIII:1, "in mother's room" & "in the pawnshop window" *Haiku International Anthology*; **Sweeney**—"Rainy season" *Acorn* 8; **Tambour**—"preoccupied" *The Heron's Nest* IV.4; **Tann**—"fumbling" *Upstate Dim Sum* 2001/1; **Tasnier**—"a few cross words" *snapshots* 9, "assertiveness class" *Presence* 16, "old love letters" *Time Haiku* 15; **Tebo**—"horsetail clouds" *South by Southeast* 9.1; **Thomann**—"jail time" *Frogpond* XXV.2; **Tico**—"With my mother gone" *Acorn* 8; **Tomé**—"open air market" *haijinx* 2.1; **Townsend**—"day's end" *The Heron's Nest* IV.10; **Trumbull**—"September chill" *Haiku Canada Newsletter* XV.3; **van den Heuvel**—"The Sunbird" *Frogpond* XXV.2; **von Sturmer**—"hot day in Kyoto" *Frogpond* XXV:2; **Vujcic**—"in prison" Kaji Aso 2002; **Weekley**—"fairy dress" *bottle rockets* 7; **Welch**—"morning sun" Drevniok 2002, "The Lotus Eaters" *Frogpond* XXV.2; **Wells**—"At the end of its leaf" *Haiku International Anthology*; **Williams**—"autumn wind" *haijinx* 2.1, "piano recital" *Blithe Spirit* 12.1; **Wyatt**—"On the telephone" *Time Haiku* 15; **Yarrow**—"lift off" *Upstate Dim Sum* 2001/2; **Yusa**—"An evening cicada" *Haiku International* 46; **Zackowitz**—"a damp evening" *haijinx* 2.1; **Zheng**—"Tangible Imagination in Richard Wright's Haiku" *Frogpond* XXV.2; **Zorman**—"my husband away" *Letni casi* 15; **Zuk**—"the harvest moon" *Modern Haiku* XXX:2.

cited sources

Books

Baranski, Johnny *Convicts Shoot the Breeze* (Normal, IL: Saki Press, 2002)
Barlow, John *Flamingo Shapes* (London: Snapshot Press, 2001)
Blundell, Colin (ed.) *FLAT* (British Haiku Society Members' Anthology 2002)
Gorman, LeRoy (ed.) *beyond spring rain* (Haiku Canada Members' Anthology 2002)
Kacian, Jim (ed.) *summer dreams* (Winchester, VA: Red Moon Press, 2002)
Savina, Zoe (ed.) *Haiku International Anthology* (Athens: Athena Press, 2002)

Periodicals

Acorn (ed. A. C. Missias, P.O. Box 186, Philadelphia PA 19105 USA)
ant ant ant ant ant (ed. chris gordon, P.O. Box 16177, Oakland CA 94610 USA)
Blithe Spirit (ed. Caroline Gourlay, Hill House Farm, Knighton Powys LD7 1NA UK)
bottle rockets (ed. Stanford M. Forrester, PO Box 290691, Wethersfield CT 06129 USA)
Frogpond (ed. Jim Kacian, PO Box 2461, Winchester VA 22604-1661 USA)
haijinx (ed. Mark Brooks, <mbrooks@haikai.info>)
Haiku Canada Newsletter (ed. LeRoy Gorman, 51 Graham West, Napanee, Ontario K7R 2J6, Canada)
Haiku Headlines (ed. David Priebe, 1347 W. 71st Street, Los Angeles CA 90044 USA)
Haiku International (Haiku International Assoc., 9-1-7-914 Akasaka, Minato-ku, Tokyo 107 Japan)
Heron's Nest, The (ed. Christopher Herold, 816 Taft St., Port Townsend WA 98368, USA)
Letni Casi (ed. Marko Hudnik, Titova 18, 4270 Jesenics, Slovenia)
Mariposa (ed. D. Claire Gallagher, 864 Elmira Drive, Sunnyvale CA 94087-1229, USA)
Mayfly (ed. Randy Brooks, 4634 Hale Drive, Decatur IL 62526 USA)
Modern Haiku (ed. Lee Gurga, Box 68, Lincoln IL 62656 USA)
Paper Wasp (ed. John Knight, 7 Bellevue Terrace, St. Lucia QLD 4067 Australia)
Presence (ed. Martin Lucas, 12 Grovehall Avenue, Leeds LS11 7EX UK)
RAW NerVZ (ed. Dorothy Howard, 67 Court Street, Aylmer (QC) J9H 4M1 Canada)
Snapshots (ed. John Barlow, PO Box 35, Sefton Park, Liverpool L17 3EG UK)
South by Southeast (ed. Steven Addiss, RC Box 93, 28 Westhampton Way, Richmond VA 23173 USA)
Starfish (ed. Irene Zahava, 307 W. State Street, Ithaca NY 14850 USA)
Still (ed. ai li, 49 Englands Lane, London Nw3 4YD UK)
Time Haiku (ed. Erica Facey, 105 Kings Head Hill, London E4 7JG UK)
Upstate Dim Sum (ed. Rt. 9 Haiku Group, PO Box 122, Nassau NY 12123 USA)
Woodpecker (ed. Wim Lofvers, Rijsterdijk 25, 8574 VW Bakhuizen, Netherlands)

Contests

The Betty Drevniok Haiku Contest 2002 (Haiku Canada)
Haiku Poets of Northern California Rengay Contest 2002
Kaji Aso Haiku Contest 2002
Kusamakura Haiku Contest 2002
Penumbra Haikuu Contest 2001 (*Penumbra* Magazine)
San Francisco International Contest: Haiku, Senryu & Tanka 2001

The RMA Editorial Staff

Jim Kacian (1996) is a co-founder of the World Haiku Association, editor of Frogpond, and owner of Red Moon Press.

Ernest J. Berry (2002) is a newcomer to haiku who feels like an old hand. He defies the reaper by refusing to write his death haiku.

Tom Clausen (1996) half accepts change yeet is always grateful for the constancy of nature, the seasons and haiku celebrating them.

Ellen Compton (1996) is a freelance writer with a background in visual and theatre arts, and a deep love for the earth.

D. Claire Gallagher (2002) Co-Editor of *Mariposa*, lives & writes on the Left Coast and laughs, hikes and gads about whenever possible.

Maureen Gorman (1997) believes her study of haiku is a perfect complement to her work as a professional counselor.

A. C. Missias (2001) is the editor of *Acorn*, past columnist for *Frogpond*, and has placed in a few haiku contests. What day job?

Kohjin Sakamoto (1997) is a university professor who has swritten haiku in English as well as Japanese for over two decades.

Alan Summers (2000) started Naked Haijin Productions so more people could know about haiku through fun transmedia projects.

George Swede (2000) works in Toronto with time out twice a year near Guadalajara.

Max Verhart (2002) is involved in haiku for over two decades and president of the Haiku Circle Netherlands since 2000.

RMA Editors-Emeritus: **Dimitar Anakiev** (2000-2001), **Janice Bostok** (1996-2001), **Dee Evetts** (1996-2001), **Lee Gurga** (1998), **Yvonne Hardenbrook** (1996-8), **John Hudak** (1996-7), **H. F. Noyes** (1996 9), **Francine Porad** (1996), **Ebba Story** (1996), **Jeff Witkin** (1996-2000).

The RMA Process

During the twelve month period December 1, 2001 through November 30, 2002, over 2000 haiku and related works by over 1500 different authors have been nominated for inclusion in *a glimpse of red: The Red Moon Anthology* 2002 by our staff of 11 editors from hundreds of sources from around the world. These sources are, in the main, the many haiku books and journals published in English, as well as the internet. Each editor is assigned a list of books and journals, but is free to nominate any work, from any source, s/he feels is of exceptional skill. In addi-tion, the editor-in-chief is responsible for reading all of these sources, which ensures every possible source is examined by at least two nominating persons.

Editors may neither nominate nor vote for their own work.

Contest winners, runners-up and honorable mentions are automatically nominated.

When the nominating period concludes, all haiku and related works which receive nomination are placed (anonymously) on a roster. The roster is then sent to each of the judges, who votes for those works s/he considers worthy of inclusion. At least 5 votes (of the 10 judges, or 50%—the editor-in-chief does not have a vote at this stage) are necessary for inclusion in the volume. The work of editors must also receive at least 5 votes from the other 9 editors (55%) to merit inclusion.

The editor-in-chief then compiles these works, seeks permissions to reprint, and assembles them into the final anthology.

Made in the USA
Monee, IL
07 July 2026

56553288R00100